strength for life's journey

Twelve-Week Spiritual Meditations
& Special Days Devotional

SHIRLEY J. INKTON BOWERS

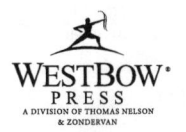

WESTBOW
PRESS
A DIVISION OF THOMAS NELSON
& ZONDERVAN

Copyright © 2015 SJInkton.

All rights reserved. No part of this book may be used or reproduced by any means, graphic, electronic, or mechanical, including photocopying, recording, taping or by any information storage retrieval system without the written permission of the publisher except in the case of brief quotations embodied in critical articles and reviews.

Scripture taken from the New King James Version. Copyright © 1979, 1980, 1982 by Thomas Nelson, Inc. Used by permission. All rights reserved.

WestBow Press books may be ordered through booksellers or by contacting:

WestBow Press
A Division of Thomas Nelson & Zondervan
1663 Liberty Drive
Bloomington, IN 47403
www.westbowpress.com
1 (866) 928-1240

Because of the dynamic nature of the Internet, any web addresses or links contained in this book may have changed since publication and may no longer be valid. The views expressed in this work are solely those of the author and do not necessarily reflect the views of the publisher, and the publisher hereby disclaims any responsibility for them.

Any people depicted in stock imagery provided by Thinkstock are models, and such images are being used for illustrative purposes only. Certain stock imagery © Thinkstock.

ISBN: 978-1-4908-7565-1 (sc)
ISBN: 978-1-4908-7566-8 (hc)
ISBN: 978-1-4908-7564-4 (e)

Library of Congress Control Number: 2015905211

Print information available on the last page.

WestBow Press rev. date: 4/16/2015

Contents

Acknowledgments ix
Preface xi
Week One 1
Week Two 11
Week Three 23
Week Four 33
Week Five 43
Week Six 53
Week Seven 63
Week Eight 73
Week Nine 83
Week Ten 95
Week Eleven 109
Week Twelve 121
New Year's Day 133
Dr. Martin Luther King, Jr. Day 135
February — Black History 136
Valentine's Day 137
Ash Wednesday 139
First Day of Lent 140
Palm Sunday 141
Easter Day 142
Mother's Day 143

Pentecost Sunday 145
Memorial Day 146
Children's Day 147
Father's Day 148
4th of July 150
Labor Day 152
Veterans Day 154
Thanksgiving Day 155
Advent 156
Christmas Day 157

> *"It is God who arms me with strength,*
> *and makes my way perfect."*
> (Psalm 18:32)

Strength for Life's Journey is dedicated in memory of my mother, Cather Mae Inkton (1926 – 2006). Because of her strength, perseverance, and faith in God, I am the woman I am today. My struggles and trials would have surely conquered my spirit, if she had not introduced me to the One in whom she put her trust. I shall forever be grateful to God for allowing me to glean from her strength for my journey.

To my jewels: Dawn, Jessica and William, my precious gifts from God. Although you are now adults, I am still humbled to be your mother. I thank you for your love, support, and encouragement.

To my dear friend Lee Ann: how I thank God for your enthusiasm, and faith in me. Thank you for encouraging me to write; and, the many gifts of journals you have given me over the years —to ensure I would not have an excuse not to.

To my family and friends, from childhood to adult; you know who you are. You saw gifts in me that I could not see. You were my spiritual safety net. When I fell, you ushered me back on my journey. Thank you for your love and prayers.

Lastly, to Larry— your strength and courage have been the inspiration behind the completion of this project. I praise God for affording me the opportunity of sharing a special part of my journey with you. Thank you for believing in me.

Acknowledgments

*S*trength for Life's Journey has been in the incubator stage for some time. The vision was conceived at my first pastoral appointment, *Quinn Chapel*; developed during my appointments to *Holly Grove, Ward Chapel, New Horizon, and Saint John;* but, God ordained the birth to take place during this season of pastoral leadership at the historical *Saint Paul African Methodist Episcopal Church*. I shall forever be grateful for the opportunity to have served as the spiritual leader of these congregations, and personally thank the members for their love and support.

Bishop Frederick H. and Dr. Sylvia R. Talbot, my Episcopal Parents in the ministry – I thank for being exceptional leaders.

Bishop Richard A. (in memoriam) and Mother Barbara J. Chappelle, Sr., – Teachers par excellence. I thank for giving me opportunities to grow in the church, and assigning my first pastoral appointment.

Bishop Samuel L. Green, Sr. – my present Episcopal leader. I thank for encouragement and the opportunities to serve.

Consultants, Rev. Sandra Smith Blair, Rev. Dr. Teresa Fry Brown, Rev. Dr. Jacquelyn Grant Collier, and Executive Board Members of African Methodist Episcopal Church Women in Ministry 2008-2012 — Serving with these ladies is an honor I will always cherish. I thank them for inspiring me to write and submit articles for publication.

Preface

This 12-week devotional is filled with wisdom that will breathe spiritual life into the thirsty soul; it serves as a conduit for strength to combat the trials life so freely distributes inclusively. Although uninvited, trials come regardless of religious affiliations, race or gender — but so do God's grace, mercy and wisdom.

In the life of the church, many may know the Word of God, and will share It verbatim from pulpit to pew; yet, we struggle with living in the reality of It. These struggles are nothing new, but because of the change in society's values, perceptions, and traditions; they may appear to be. In general, the majority of Christians don't share their struggles with their pastor, or other members of their congregation because of the "trust" factor. The family relationship that once existed in the church is slowly dissipating— people are finding it easier to stay home. It is my prayer, as you meditate on these devotions, your hope, faith, and trust in God, as well as the church, will be renewed.

We all could use a little encouragement from time to time. These inspirational nuggets hold the key to growth and revitalization needed to help us on our spiritual journeys. In the words of the great Harlem Renaissance poet Langston Hughes, "Life for me ain't been no crystal stair." Many of us can attest to this sentiment; however, we must remember, it is God who gives us the strength we need as we travel through life's journey.

WEEK ONE

Day One

"—Men always ought to pray and not lose heart."
(Luke 18:1)

What an awesome God we serve, and what a blessing and privilege it is to call upon our Creator at all times! We never have to worry about God's line being busy or out-of-order. We don't even have to worry about having our calls monitored by God's caller-ID. And praise the Lord; we don't have to go through a computerized answering service intercepting our calls. Our prayers are really very important to our Father, and He looks forward to the intimacy they bring.

Jesus tells us that we should always pray, regardless of how our circumstances may appear; prayer changes things. There is no power stronger than the power of prayer because this is when we connect to the true power source, almighty God; we know nothing is too hard for God.

When it seems like Murphy's Law desires to become your new best friend, just pray; when your plans don't work out, just pray. When it seems the weight of the world is weighing you down and peace of mind cannot be found, just pray and don't lose heart. God wants to hear from you, but not just in tough times: in good times too. God is just a prayer away.

Day Two

"But the just shall live by his faith."
(Habakkuk 2:4)

We have heard the proverb, "Where there is no vision, the people perish" *(Proverbs 29:18—KJV)*, but do we believe these words to be evident and true? One way we can honestly answer this question is by evaluating our own personal hopes and dreams. Visions are often looked upon as long-ranged, something yet to come. Where do you see yourself five years from now? What plans have you made to achieve your goals? In other words, what are you working on right now that will ensure your vision comes to fruition?

What about the church in which your name is on the roll? How do you visualize it in five years? It is my prayer that you have envisioned a flourishing and vibrant church ministering to the needs of God's people. What steps are you taking right now to help make this vision a reality?

Please be aware of a dangerous silent killer in our midst. It breeds apathy in our personal lives as well as our churches; its name is Complacency. It lures us into our comfort zones and robs us of all desires for initiating change. Whether in our personal lives or the church, if change for the better is not taking place, death is inevitable.

Allow me to encourage you to dream dreams of what can be, but in the same vein, don't forget you must be willing to do your part if you expect your dreams to become reality. Yes, the just shall live by faith, but remember, faith without works is dead *(James 2:17)*.

Day Three

*"This is the day the Lord has made;
we will rejoice and be glad in it."*
(Psalm 118:24)

What a precious blessing God has bestowed upon us: the blessing of seeing another day. By God's grace, we have been given another chance to do that which we should have done yesterday. Because of God's love, we have been given the power and authority to let our lights so shine that our good works may glorify and lead others to our matchless Father. And if you have not truly committed your life to Christ, you have been afforded another opportunity to reconnect to the true Vine. Yes, Christ knows each one of our hearts; there is nothing that can be hidden from Him. The beauty of it is — He loves us in spite of our faults and failures. What an awesome God we serve!

Today is your day to rejoice in the Lord. Today is your day to recommit your life to Christ. Today is your day to surrender your will to the Lord's will. He has great plans for you, but you must be willing to accept Him first. Try God — you'll be glad you did.

Day Four

*"And Elisha prayed, and said, 'Lord, I pray,
open his eyes that he may see'."*
(2 Kings 6:17)

One sure way to stunt spiritual growth is to walk by earthly insight and not by godly faith. Allowing what we see with our earthly eyes to dictate our action or pre-determine the outcome of our efforts is sight-based faith walking. This is not faith in God but faith in our ability and strength to make something happen.

Jesus instructs His disciples in Mark 11:22 to have faith in God, and He assures them, as well as us today, that we have been given mountain-moving faith if only we believe that God is able to do what we ask in prayer.

The greater our faith, the greater the miracles God will allow us to witness. The above Scripture describes a faith that reveals God's unfailing faithfulness to one who had great faith in God (Elisha). And because Elisha's servant was yet blind to the spiritual reality of God's power, this opportunity was used to help him see through spiritual eyes. With the natural eye, all that the servant could see was the mighty Syrian army had surrounded the city of Dothan in search of God's prophet, but Elisha prayed, asking God to allow the young man to see the far more mighty and powerful army of horses and chariots of fire that God had sent to protect him. The result — God struck the Syrian army with physical blindness, and instead of the army capturing one man, one God-fearing man captured the army.

If you are looking for a miracle, walk with expectancy and act upon your faith in God.

Day Five

"Let your light so shine before men, that they may see your good works and glorify your Father in heaven."
(Matthew 5:16)

Our lives are walking and talking books of who we really are and what we really believe. It has been said that the life that a Christian lives "could be" the only testament to God—the only Bible—the unsaved may read. Have you ever thought about what your life really says about your faith in God, love for God's people, and obedience to God's will?

We are living in perilous times. Chaos is all around us; some even believe we're in the last days. Now more than ever, Christians must step up to the plate and put on the whole armor of God *(Ephesians 6:11)*. If we are to glorify God, we must be seen in the proper context: we must be found being about our Father's business constantly, and twenty-four seven, our lights must be shining brightly so that others will see who we really are, not by our words but by our actions. Only by doing this, Jesus said, would we glorify our Father in heaven.

Allow me to encourage you to assess the life that you are presently living. Does it glorify God or flesh? Remember, the lives that we live do bear witness of what we truly believe. Let me put it another way: our actions do speak much louder than our words.

Day Six

*"For it is better, if it is the will of God,
to suffer for doing good than for doing evil."*
(1 Peter 3:17)

Why do good (righteous) people have to suffer? This question has been pondered from generation to generation, yet we have not been able to find a satisfying answer.

Can you think of a martyr who didn't suffer for a noble cause? I believe the philosophy of martyrs may have been as follows: the need of many outweigh the need of one. Therefore, giving up their lives was worth the many lives that would benefit from their sacrifice.

In reality, no one wants to suffer; however, there are times in our lives when we find ourselves doing just that, and many times we suffer for doing what's right in the eyes of God.

The greatest martyr who ever lived is known as the suffering servant; He humbled Himself and accepted the will of God. He carried the sins of the world to the cross on Calvary, and because of this awesome sacrifice, we were reconciled to our Father.

If you are experiencing the pain of suffering and it is because of your efforts to do God's will, be not dismayed: the Father will take care of you. Remember: if God brought you to it, God will bring you through it.

Day Seven

*"Those who trust in the Lord are like Mount Zion,
which cannot be moved, but abides forever."*
(Psalm 125:1)

When you think of the word *mountain*, what comes to mind? Mountains can be symbolic of massive and insurmountable challenges that are very difficult to overcome. They come in all shapes, forms, and fashions.

Another important question is how do we react to mountains? Some may enter into a stage of denial, pretending the mountain does not exist; therefore, business as usual is the answer (conformers). Others may tend to take matters into their own hands, believing the mountain has intruded upon their turf; therefore, they will use whatever means necessary to get rid of it (controllers). Then there are those who might decide that the cause just isn't worth the headache of confronting the mountain; consequently, they pack up their belongings and hike out in another direction (cowards).

As Christians, we mustn't fall into any of the above categories because they all focus on the self. Our desire should always be to do that which will please God because our existence is for God's glory, not ours. If we seek God's will first, God will supply us with everything we need to deal with our mountains.

Now my last question is one I pray you will feast upon. Do *you* trust in God? If your answer is yes, God's Word says you are equivalent to a mountain, Mount Zion to be exact, symbolic to the place in which God dwells. Those who trust in God embrace the mountain (conquerors).

WEEK TWO

Day One

"—But time and chance happen to them all."
(Ecclesiastes 9:11)

If you are reading this, God has given you another opportunity to take part in a new year. Although, in the Bible the Preacher writes that nothing under the sun is new *(Ecclesiastes 1:9)*, we understand that he speaks of the concept, not the experience. For example, most of us have seen many New Years come and go; however, each one was different, but yet the same. The commonalities could be inclusive of each beginning consistently with the month of January and ending with December— the differences could be the experiences or happenings that took place during each day of each month. To simplify it even more, no matter how many beautiful babies are born, each one's arrival brings new life; this is why we affectionately call them "newborns."

The words penned by Solomon the Preacher also teaches us to be mindful of the time that God allows us to embrace, for there is a time for every purpose under the heaven *(3:11)*. Let us remember time and chance as they relate to earth and heaven. On earth, the swift wins the race, the strong wins the battle, and accolades are given to the skilled. In heaven, we are rewarded for our faithfulness to God; the time we commit to serving God and the use of the spiritual gifts God so freely gives us for Christ's glory.

It is my prayer that we each will embark upon this year with new dreams, new hopes, and a renewed commitment to God. Let us not take chances with our souls' salvation.

Day Two

*"—he knelt down on his knees . . .
and prayed and gave thanks before his God"*
(Daniel 6:10)

The power of prayer is as unexplainable as the goodness of God, but they both are real. So many times we allow circumstances to disturb our lives because we either forget or fail to pray.

Prayer was no stranger to Daniel; the Bible reveals that it was his custom to pray three times daily. This was a time he not only looked forward to but held in reverence.

Unfortunately, sometimes our relationship with God can bring attention and cause haters to attack our character for the sole purpose of seeking self-glory, as with the story of Daniel. We must learn to trust God even more when these tests come. Instead of reacting to destructive traps, we must pray for God's power to be seen in the midst of persecution. Daniel was placed in the lions' den because of his relationship with God, but the God in whom he believed, prayed and trusted, sent an angel to shut the lions' mouths — and as fate would have it, Daniel's haters were literally fed to the lions (6:24).

From this day forward, remember the power of prayer; and use it to bring glory to God. I am a firm and avid believer that God still answers "knee mail."

Day Three

"Ask, and it shall be given to you; Seek, and you shall find; Knock, and it shall be opened to you."
(Matthew 7:7—KJV)

Have you ever noticed that the first letter of each word that Jesus tells us to do in Matthew 7:7 spells out the word "ASK"?

Because of the spirit of pride (which rests in all of us to some degree), it becomes very difficult to ask for help, even when we really need it. We've heard, or may have even uttered these words: "I had to swallow my pride and ask" or, "In desperation, I had to ask." For Christians, we tend to have an even greater challenge with this asking concept; it is as though someone taught us that because we are followers of Christ, everything would be given to us on a silver platter, but this is not what Jesus teaches in the above Scripture.

We learn not to be afraid, intimidated, or prideful when it comes to **A**sking God and others for what we desire, especially if it's for the edification of God's church, or even our personal needs. We must diligently **S**eek to find the desires of our hearts in unusual places; and **K**nock on every door of opportunity that we encounter.

Meditate on this thought. Marriage is one of the most sacred institutions ordained by God; yet, it could not exist without one *asking* another.

Step out in faith and "ASK" today.

Day Four

"No weapon formed against you shall prosper—"
(Isaiah 54:17)

When my spirit is broken and I find it difficult to get a glimpse of light at the end of the very long tunnel that I am traveling, I often turn to the 54th chapter of Isaiah. There I find solace and encouragement for my soul. Along this Christian journey, I've found that walking in the steps that God orders isn't always the easiest task to accept. As a matter of fact, it can be downright difficult. It is during these times that I remind myself of God's awesome love. How difficult it must have been for God the Father to send His only Son into a world that He already knew would reject and demand His life; yet, Jesus accepted this task, which was accompanied by pain and loneliness in the name of Love—love for us.

Many weapons were formed against Jesus, with the most powerful one being that of death, but even the grave could not prosper in holding Him; for it was on that 3rd day that He arose with all power in heaven and earth in His hands.

We must learn to encourage ourselves in God's Word every day, and remember our steps are tailor-made just for each one of us individually. I can't walk in yours and you can't walk in mine. It is our Father who has assigned us the tasks that He knows we can perform, but we must be willing to accept what God allows in our lives in order for our purpose and mission to be fulfilled. This may mean going it alone, and temporarily accepting rejection and pain as traveling companions—however, the day will come when God rewards us openly for our faithfulness and obedience to Him.

Remember, weapons may form, but only God's Word will prosper.

Day Five

"—But who do you say that I am?"
(Matthew 16:15)

It is seldom that you run upon a person who has not heard of Jesus, especially here in the United States. Most religions have their own interpretation as to who He is. But more importantly, the question that comes to mind is "who is Jesus to us?" (those who profess to be His followers).

Jesus asked this thought-provoking question of His disciples, and only one out of the twelve was able to reveal His true identity, by the grace of God. The other disciples were able to repeat what they had heard others call Him (John, Elijah, Jeremiah, a prophet), but when it came down to their own personal faith, they were all tongue-tied.

If we are to lead others to Christ, we must first be able to personally testify of His majesty. It is impossible to testify on behalf of someone or something that we do not know to be real or true. The only way this can be done is through a personal relationship with Him.

I challenge you this day to have faith in Christ; trust Him to do something in your life that you know only He could do. And when Christ shows up and shows out, be a witness: let your testimony of His power, love and greatness be as strong as the winds of a hurricane. Make sure God gets ALL of the glory.

Day Six

"Hear the word of the LORD. *Thus says the* LORD: *'Tomorrow about this time a seah of fine flour shall be sold for a shekel—' So a seah of fine flour was sold for a shekel— according to the word of the* LORD."
(2 Kings 7:1 & 16)

What a difference a day makes! Some would call this an old cliché, but I believe there is truth in its substance.

In the 6th chapter of 2 Kings, we find the capital of Israel, Samaria, undergoing a most horrific famine because of their disrespect and disobedience to God. This famine was so drastic that some stooped to cannibalism. To say the least, hope was nowhere to be found; only gloom, doom, despair and death.

The Word of the Lord, sent via His servant Elisha, brought good news. In his proclamation, it was revealed that God would provide an abundant amount of food for the people the very next day. We know that God's Word is infallible— it did come to pass.

There are many different types of famines that plague our lives today (famines of family, friends, finances, peace, and love, to name a few). It is very likely that if you have not already experienced some type of famine, you just might in the future.

Receive these words of encouragement: God can change your situation in the blink of an eye. Regardless of how dismal or impossible things may appear in the natural realm, never forget that God is able to do exceedingly abundantly above all that we can ask, think or imagine. Don't lose hope.

Day Seven

"For He Himself is our peace— and has broken down the middle wall of separation . . ."
(Ephesians 2:14)

Walls, visible or invisible, can denote separation and/or protection. They are either meant to keep one in or out for various reasons; but in most cases, they represent a fear of what uninvited change will bring. Fear of the unknown can be one of our worst enemies because the adversary feeds off and uses it to usher enmity (hostility) into our lives.

Adam and Eve were inside the symbolic walls of Utopia; God protected them, and they had no need of anything because everything had been abundantly supplied. Unfortunately, they feared they were missing out on something; and their ill-choice allowed enmity to enter into the world and separate them from God *(Genesis 3)*.

Yes, the walls of segregation, degradation and humiliation still exist. There are those who cannot feel up-lifted unless they are bringing others down; but, the Word of God reminds us if we are in Christ, we are one *(Galatians 3:28)*. If we can receive this Word, we must also know that regardless of the walls, our peace comes from knowing just how much we are loved by Christ; for it was Christ who reconciled us to the Father through the cross, thusly, putting to death enmity *(Ephesians 2:16)*.

In spite of the challenges you are facing right now, be encouraged and remember that no walls shall separate you from the love of God, which is in Christ Jesus. *"Though Satan should buffet, though trials should come, let this blest assurance control, that Christ has regarded my helpless estate, and has shed His own blood for my soul."* **(H.G. Spafford)**

WEEK THREE

Day One

*"Delight yourself also in the Lord, and He shall
give you the desires of your heart."*
(Psalms 37:4)

God the Father has given us another opportunity to allow God the Son to show us just what He wants to do for us through God the Holy Spirit.

We are challenged to seek God's glory. As a matter of fact, the Lord waits patiently for us to give Him a chance to show Himself strong in our lives. But we ask ourselves, "what is God waiting for us to do— Pray?" Praying is a good thing, but that's not what God is waiting for; the Lord is patiently waiting for us to delight ourselves in Him. To delight ourselves in the Lord means to establish not only a prayer relationship, but a love relationship; yes, an intimate love affair with God. The Lord desires for us to take great joy and pleasure in His presence and spend time with Him daily. This means: studying the Word of God, communing and listening as God speaks to us; trusting and obeying His will for our lives. We should possess a passion for seeking new ways to highly please and praise God. It is when we open our hearts to the Lord, in such a passionate manner, He inhabits our delight and releases every good and perfect gift that we desire. God even takes pleasure in giving us desires of our hearts that we don't even know we have.

Don't take my word, try delighting yourself in the Lord— and watch how He proves His Word is true over and over again in your life.

Day Two

"—I am with you always, even to the end of the age."
(Matthew 28:20)

*Y*ou may have read or even have a copy of the popular poem entitled, "Footprints" by Mary Stevenson. It tells of a man who had gone through some very difficult trials in life, but he knew Jesus was right there with him every step of the way because of His footprints in the sand. The man's concern came during the most difficult times of his life, for it was then that he noticed there was only one set of footprints. Curious, he asked Jesus why was it that when he needed Him the most he had to walk alone. Jesus told the man that where he saw only one set of prints were the times that He had carried him; therefore, the footprints that the man had witnessed were those of Jesus.

There are times in our lives when we feel that our burdens, trials, and tribulations are too much to bear. We, like the man in the poem, sometimes may even feel as though Jesus has abandoned us, but He hasn't. It is in those times that we must remember Jesus promised to be with us "always." Jesus promised to never leave nor forsake us *(Heb. 13:5)*, and in the Gospel of John *(10:28)*, He promised that no one would ever be able to take us away or separate us from Him.

Beloved, there are many things that I do not know, but there is one thing I truly believe— God is a promise keeper. Allow me to encourage you this day to always remember, regardless of how things may appear, God is *always* with you, *even to the end of the age.*

Day Three

"As for God, His way is perfect; the Word of the Lord is proven; He is a shield to all who trust in Him."
(Psalm 18:30)

Will you testify with me to the strength and substance of the psalmist's words above? God's way is truly perfect. Even though God's ways are definitely not like ours *(Isaiah 55:8-9)*, and we don't always understand, it is still our duty to embrace them with faith, for God knows our end from our beginning.

In my life, God's Word has been proven over and over again. There have been times when I was close to giving up, but God stepped in at just the right time to lift me up. Many dangerous toils and snares have been flung my way, but God has kept me; God has been a shield for me because I put my trust in Him.

I personally want you to know that God is not a respecter of person, for if Christ looked passed all of my faults; saw and fulfilled my needs, He will do the same for you. The key element is you must trust God.

Many times we fail to receive the blessings God wants to give us because we are too busy trying to fix our own problems. There is substance, strength, and power in God's Word, but only those who truly trust God will experience them *(Proverbs 3:5-6)*. Are you a witness? The answer to this question can be found in your everyday faith-walk.

Day Four

"For God so loved the world that He gave His only begotten Son, that whoever believes in Him should not perish but have everlasting life."
(John 3:16)

The book of Ecclesiastes speaks of seasons, times and purposes. It begins with the natural event of human life, "a time to be born and a time to die." In God's love for us, He gave His one and only sin-less Son to be born into a world of sin. In God's wisdom, the perfect time had been set and foretold for Christ's majestic arrival *(Isaiah 11:1-2 & 9:6-7)*. And because of God's grace and mercy toward His children, the purpose of Jesus' coming has been clearly stated, "I have come that they may have life, and that they may have it more abundantly."*(John 10:10)* To sum it all up, Jesus brought to us the gift of salvation. Because of His awesome sacrifice: the shedding of His precious blood and taking our place on the cross; we have been given the opportunity of accepting this priceless gift— but each one of us must choose for ourselves. It's all about choices. Gifts do us no good unless we choose to use them for the purpose they were given. For example, if you were given the gift of a car but you never used it, what good would it be to you?

We have not been promised tomorrow, but God has allowed us to see this day; what shall we do with it?

There is a purpose for this season and time in your life; do you know what it is? If not, the Holy Spirit will help you *(John 14:26)*.

Be encouraged, God loves you just as you are. Believe in Him whom the Father sent; accept the Gift of salvation that has been given to you, and receive everlasting life.

Day Five

"Call to Me, and I will answer you, and show you great and mighty things, which you do not know."
(Jeremiah 33:3)

If we learn very little during the time that God allows us to live in this world, it is imperative that we learn to trust God more and more each day. Our trust in God's love, realness, and omnipotence is what gets us through each trial, tribulation, and challenge that we face. As children of God, we must begin to trust more and think less, if we really believe that the Lord is the Author and Finisher of our faith.

As with each new day, challenges as well as opportunities await us. I am a firm believer that challenges are the God's way of reminding us of the Holy Spirit's presence, power and grace; however, it is unfortunate if we only call upon our Maker when trouble arises.

God wants to show us "great and mighty things," but it is up to us whether or not we want to see them. We have God's Word and know that it is impossible for God to lie *(Numbers 23:19)*. We acknowledge and believe that God is able to do exceedingly abundantly above all that we can ask or think *(Ephesians 3:20)*. And we know that God is willing, for we are encouraged to call to God in the above Scripture— God promises to answer.

Before you begin or end your day, it is my prayer that you will leave whatever may be hindering your faith and trust at the altar of our most high God.

Day Six

*"—'I have been zealous for the Lord God of hosts . . .
I alone am left; and they seek to take my life.'"*
(1 Kings 19:10 & 14)

Have you ever been directed by the Holy Spirit to do something that could actually bring havoc to your life?

In the above scripture, we find the prophet Elijah in such a predicament. God had used Elijah in miraculous ways to speak on God's behalf, but somehow the fear factor slipped into his spirit and he finds himself running for his life because he's on Jezebel's "hit list". Elijah had a brain freeze. He forgot in Whom he put his trust. He forgot the One in whom he was serving; he forgot that it was God that had been working through him. God had used him to proclaim a drought in the land and bring embarrassment upon the prophets of the idol god, Baal. Even so, Elijah feared for his life.

As human beings, in our finite wisdom, we are fragile; sometimes even fickle and forgetful. Our faith is often challenged after attacks are deplored against us. Yes, our faith of yesterday seems to have gone on vacation, or maybe even hiding in the corridors of our minds; but if our faith fails us, our memory shouldn't. The Word tells us that Christ is the same yesterday, today, and forever *(Hebrews 13:8)*. The same Christ that was with us on yesterday will protect, provide, and empower us for the challenges of today.

God will never leave you alone.

Day Seven

*"My soul magnifies the Lord,
and my spirit has rejoiced in God my Savior."*
(Luke 1:46-47)

How do we respond to God's calling in our lives? Does it depend upon the calling? If it's easy, do we say "yes"? If it's difficult, do we say "no" or "let me think about it"?

Mary accepted the possibility of gross embarrassment, not only to her, but to her loved ones as well. God chose her to usher in the Savior of humanity, to give birth to our Immanuel (God with us). This could have been a difficult call for Mary, as she wasn't married—engaged, but not married, plus she was a virgin. What would people think? What would people say? She could have pondered these questions and responded to God with the words, "let me think about it." But she didn't. Her response was, "Let it be to me according to your word." Mary had made plans for her life, but she accepted God's plans instead. She didn't know what the outcome would be, but she trusted God and rejoiced in His favor towards her.

We too, must understand that our plans for our lives and God's plans may not always align, but if we take on the attitude of Mary, trust God, and say "yes," we'll also witness God's miraculous power. Remember, we were made for God's purpose, not vice-versa.

WEEK FOUR

Day One

"Do not remember the former things, nor consider the things of old. Behold, I will do a new thing—"
(Isaiah 43:18-19)

When my interest turned toward learning to drive an automobile, I was told by the wise it would be to my advantage to learn how to drive a standard gear shift first, instead of an automatic; but I chose the easy way of attaining my desire. Everything was fine until I bought my very 1st 'nice' car, an Acura Legend, which had a standard gear shift. What a challenge!!! The fact being, the car wasn't hard to drive; however, my mindset was the problem. It was difficult for me to hold on to what I had learned about the mechanics of driving and turn loose of the knowledge that was no longer applicable. I guess I could say, because of my previous learning, it was difficult for me to literally 'shift gears" but after much practice, I did.

This analogy reminds me of our Christian journey. So many times we choose to take the easier path of service; we depend on those ahead of us to carry our cross, as well as their own— then, one day, we wake up and realize that they are no longer there. The choice becomes crucial. Will we follow in their footsteps? Will we shift gears and pick up where they left off, or will we continue in an automated state of self-desire?

Day Two

*"The blessing of the Lord makes one rich,
And He adds no sorrow with it."*
(Proverbs 10:22)

Have you ever taken the time to count your blessings? The writer of the above Scripture reminds us the blessings God sends make us wealthy. This "wealth" is not reflective of just monetary things, but everything our hearts desires. There is a pre-requisite; we must be guided by the Word and Spirit of God, delighting ourselves first in the Father (who is the Giver of every good and perfect gift, *—James 1:17*); then, wait patiently for God to give us our hearts' desires *(Psalm 37:4-5)*. It is only at this point that we are able to truly appreciate what we have been given. In submission to God's will, God's desires for us become our desires for ourselves.

Be encouraged, for the blessings of the Lord make us rich in the spirit of joy and gratitude. Just take a few minutes to reflect on the Lord's blessings; remembering the joy that flooded your soul in response to God hearing and answering your past prayers.

Instead of dwelling on what you don't have, I admonish you to turn your attention to what you have been given. In other words, count your blessings!

Day Three

*"Oh give thanks to the Lord! Call upon His Name;
Make known His deeds among the peoples!"*
(1 Chronicles 16:8)

God is worthy of our praise, our worship, and our gratitude. Thanking God should not be an afterthought, it should be as natural as breathing, for when we think about how good God has been to us individually and collectively, our souls should look back and wonder, just why God loves us so. It is when we forget to thank God for His many benefits that our hearts become cold and we began to take credit for all of our accomplishments.

Today, we have been given another opportunity to be a witness for God. We can start by sharing the miracles God has performed in our lives with others. Let us make known God's deeds to those who may not know God's love or power. In doing so, I encourage you to expect God to perform even greater miracles in your life. Remember, God inhabits the praises of His people —this is why we believe "When praises go up— blessings come down!"

Day Four

"Is anything too hard for the Lord?"
(Genesis 18:14)

Why is it we often put God into a box that is big enough to only hold our analytical thoughts? In other words, why do we so often measure God's ability by our own human standards?

In the above Scripture, the Lord asks Abraham, "Is there anything too hard for the Lord?" after Sarah laughed at the absurd thought of her giving birth to a child in her old age; in the natural, it was no longer humanly possible for Sarah to bear children— But we serve a supernatural God, who chose to make a believer out of her with the miracle pregnancy and birth of Isaac.

God specializes in miracles. Miracles are those blessings that show up in our lives that cannot be explained. In our human understanding, they should not exist; our analytical thoughts are at a lost.

God wants all of us to experience miracles, but we must be willing to step out by faith, believing that no matter how difficult or impossible our situation may appear, "with God all things are possible." *(Matt. 19:26)*

Day Five

"For the Lord God is a sun and shield; the Lord will give grace and glory; no good thing will He withhold from those who walk uprightly."
(Psalm 84:11)

How's your walk with God?
The psalmist pens in the 10th verse of the 84th Psalm; one day in the presence of God is better than one thousand days absent of God. What an awesome thought!

Walking with God on a daily basis is as important to the living as breathing; for it is when we walk with God that we experience the full benefits of God's Fatherly protection, care, and provisions.

One of our favorite sayings is: "God knows my heart"—this is true, and our hearts can be seen through our everyday walk in God's presence. The above Scripture tells us God gives favor (grace) and His glory (anointing) to those who walk uprightly. It is spiritually impossible to walk upright without walking in the presence of God the Holy Spirit.

Let us practice walking with God on a daily basis —"Let your light so shine …"

Day Six

"The people who are with you are too many— lest Israel claim glory for itself against Me"
(Judges 7:2)

There's an old adage, "One plus the Lord is a majority." For those who must be able to reason or logically deduce everything, this saying is simply bogus and does not compute. Their focus is more on the "one" and human frailty. They forget, or maybe just don't know, the Lord is a majority without the "one." Furthermore, the "one" finds favor because the Lord is on his or her side.

In the 7th chapter of Judges, God speaks to Gideon through an angel and sends him on a mission to war against the Midianites. Logically deducing this assignment, it doesn't make sense. Gideon, first of all, acknowledges that he not only was a descendant from the weakest tribe (Manasseh), but he was also the least of his father's house. I guess he thought God did not know these things. Even while Gideon was hiding out in the winepress threshing wheat, God had deemed him a "mighty man of valor" *(Judges 6:12)*. Through the process of elimination, God ordered Gideon to utilize only 300 of the original approximately 32,000 men who actually went into battle. God's aim was to make sure no flesh would become hoodwinked into thinking they (the Israelites) won the victory in their own strength— the glory for this victory was to be God's alone.

Today, let us not become so overwhelmed by scientific laws of nature that we forget the One who made nature. There is nothing too hard for God, and even now, God still chooses to make His glory known through the remnants and least likely people and situations of this world. Don't look to numbers for power. Look to God.

Day Seven

*"So he made haste and came down
and received Him joyfully."*
(Luke 19:6)

Have you ever stopped to think about what makes you happy? Just what is it that tickles your fancy? What really excites you?

During the winter season, many become excited about the Super Bowl game. Preparations are made; parties are thrown. Special foods are purchased, friends and family are invited over to watch the game, and in some instances, bets are placed. Many people get really excited about this annual day, but what about the day after? Super Bowls come once a year, and they only last a few hours; the excitement is temporary. Wouldn't it be wonderful to get excited about something that lasts forever?

In the 19th chapter of Luke, we find a story that exemplifies the ultimate excitement one could experience— the joy of finding Jesus. Even though Zacchaeus had to climb up a tree to get a glimpse, Jesus saw his heart and was well pleased. Because of the attitude of excitement, joy, and repentance Zacchaeus displayed, Jesus brought salvation to his household.

We too should be excited, and full of joy, for the salvation that God gave to us through His one and only son, Jesus. If we can't get excited about the gift of eternal life, what in this world can save us?

WEEK FIVE

Day One

"Be strong and of good courage"
(Joshua 1:6)

The fore-parents of African Americans saw God move in mysterious ways. Although many were born into slavery, they believed God had the power to free them from their bonds, first spiritually then physically — and God did, but not without a struggle. If we were to give the "struggle" a name I believe it would be called "Change."

The implication of change can often be our worst enemy because it causes us to do things differently and this usually takes us out of our comfort zones. These uncomfortable feelings have been known to produce resentment, fear, and even chaos.

The Civil war came into being as a result of change. The Southern states feared losing their slaves so much that they were willing to fight against the law of the land to keep them. They were living in a self-righteous world, even using the Bible to defend their beliefs as it related to owning slaves. Because of their resistance to change, many lives were lost, but in the end, God spoke and slavery, as it had been known, was abolished.

It takes strength and "good courage" to submit to God's will in becoming an instrument of change. I believe Joshua, who God chose as Moses' successor, would attest to this. In this 21st century, we must remember the torch must be passed on from generation to generation, if all people and the Church are to survive and provide for our posterity greater opportunities in life.

Day Two

*"I am the vine, you are the branches. He who abides
in Me, and I in him, bears much fruit;
for without Me you can do nothing."*
(John 15:5)

Are you connected to the true Power source? What would happen if we didn't plug our appliances, televisions and computers into electrical sockets? It really wouldn't matter how new or beautiful these items may be; the most we would get from them would be, perhaps a good conversation piece. We would not be able to witness the efficiency of them, or their effectiveness. Even though they may have names that specify what they are, they would not be able to function in the required capacity because the one source that makes them operate is missing: POWER. This same principle holds true for us, as Christians. Without a personal relationship with Jesus, we are limited in every aspect of our lives. We may exist, but can do nothing without Him.

Do you desire to be a witness for God? Plug into Jesus! Do you want to bask in the power and glory of the Trinity? Plug into Jesus!! Do you want your light to shine in a way that others may see your good works and glorify your Father? Plug into Jesus!!! Remember, Jesus is the true Power source.

Day Three

*"Oh, how great is Your goodness— which you
have prepared for those who trust in You
in the presence of the sons of men!"*
(Psalm 31:19)

The goodness of God is unexplainable; nothing compares with God's favor. But to experience just how great God's goodness really is, the psalmist says we must trust in God in the presence of the sons of men. In other words, the more we demonstrate our trust, belief, and hope in God when in the company of others, the greater God's goodness will be in our lives.

Have you ever thought about the amount of time you spend witnessing to others about God's blessings in your life? Do you believe that it's important to tell about the goodness of God to people outside of the church, or are you ashamed and/or uncomfortable sharing the God that you serve with others?

Jesus said whoever is ashamed of Him and His Words in this world, He will be ashamed of when He returns in the glory of His Father with the angels *(Mark 8:38)*. I surely don't want my Lord and Savior to be ashamed of me now or when He returns. Nothing gives me more joy than sharing God's goodness with others.

Be encouraged this day to share the Good News of Jesus Christ with others. Don't be selfish; if we are to love our neighbors as ourselves, we must learn to share with others as freely as God shares with us.

Day Four

"—But the just shall live by his faith."
(Habakkuk 2:4)

Faith is an awe-inspiring word, but an even more powerful action.

My eyes have been opened to a revelation that for some reason I missed seeing for years. As I prayed and meditated about what God would have me to pen concerning this gift of "Faith," I was inspired to review the concordance of the Bible. I've viewed a significant number of Scriptures on faith many times before, yet this time, I saw something I had missed. The term, **faith**, became alive through Jesus Christ. All of the Scriptures I found using the word 'faith' were in the New Testament from Matthew to Revelations, with the exceptions of Deuteronomy 32:20 and Habakkuk, as noted above. I am not a scholar, so I may have missed one or two, but even so, the implications behind faith being instilled as such a necessary part of Christian living should shake us all.

Jesus instituted the concept of faith through not only Word, but also action. He taught us the importance of living by faith. And by faith, Jesus went to the cross on our behalf.

What does this say to us today? The answer can be found in our daily walk with God— For we walk by faith . . . *(2 Corinthians 5:7)*. But without faith it is impossible to please God (Hebrews 11:6).

Day Five

*"All Your works shall praise You, O Lord,
And Your saints shall bless You."*
(Psalm 145:10)

Have you ever taken the time to witness the glory of the Lord? From the rising of the sun to the going down of the same, our God is worthy of our praise and worship. I concur with King David in Psalm 8:4, *"What is man that You are mindful of him and the sons and daughters of man that You visit them?"* (paraphrased) When I just think about the majestic universe, in which God created and the beautiful habitation on it, my soul can't help but shout hallelujah! And when I think about all of the important matters God has to attend; yet, He takes the time to be concerned about me, I can't hold back the tears; I can't help but praise God more and more. For our God is the God of all grace; regardless of how hopeless our situations may appear, we have the blessed assurance that God's grace is sufficient for our every need.

    I challenge you today to begin praising God for His mighty works. You may want to begin by just praising Him for what He's done in your personal life, but don't stop there. Praise God for His goodness and mercy. Praise God for loving the world so much that He gave His only begotten Son. Praise God for Jesus. In Jesus' name, "Let everything that has breath praise the Lord!"

Day Six

"—Whatever things are true, whatever things are noble, whatever things are just, whatever things are pure, whatever things are of a good report— meditate on these things."
(Philippians 4:8)

What's on your mind? God's Word instructs us to meditate on things that are: true, noble, just, pure, good, and praiseworthy in the world around us. In times like these it is important to not only remember, but to keep these instructions in our hearts. If God's peace is to reign sovereign in our lives, we must remember that it is up to each one of us to renew our spirits daily. I believe this is why the Apostle Paul admonished the Church at Rome to be careful not to conform to the values and ways of this world, but to be transformed by the renewing of their minds *(Romans 12:2)*. A mind dedicated to the wrongs of this secular world will produce a life tossed back and forth by the currents of culture. But a mind that is dedicated to God's truth will produce a life that can stand the test of time.

Our lives should reflect we are truly set apart for God's great plan of salvation; our reasonable service is to present our bodies, our wills, our minds, and our hearts to God as living sacrifices. Though the vicissitudes of life are very present in our midst, if our minds are stayed on God, we will be kept in perfect peace (Isaiah 26:3).

Day Seven

*"The steps of a good man are ordered by the Lord,
and He delights in his way."*
(Psalm 37:23)

One of my favorite childhood poems is Robert Frost's, "*The Road Not Taken*." It reveals the necessity to sometimes choose roads or take on challenges that others have not; it also reminds us of our purpose to fulfill our destiny.

King David reminds us that God orders the steps of those who profess to be His followers. In doing so, we find ourselves walking down paths that others would not walk, but we have the assurance our Father would never lead us down a road that He had not already prepared for us to walk. The path we take may be filled with the unknown, but it is our Christian duty to remember that we walk by faith and not by sight (2 Corinthians 5:7).

Let me encourage you today with this thought — the Word of God won't lead you where the grace of God can't keep you. No matter how disillusioned you may become with the path you're taking, remember, if it is the Lord who is ordering your steps, your blessing awaits you, because God delights in your ways.

WEEK SIX

Day One

*"For the Lord is great and greatly to be praised;
He is also to be feared above all gods."*
(1 Chronicles 16:25)

If a poll were to be taken today, how great would your praise and testimony of God measure up?

Jesus teaches in Matthew 5:14-15 that we are reflectors of God's light; therefore, as we behold the glory of the Lord in our lives, it is our responsibility to praise and testify of His mighty works, so others will be drawn to God's marvelous light.

The writer of 1 Chronicles reminds us in the above Scripture that not only is God great and should be No. 1 on our praise list, but also, we must be careful to honor God above all other gods.

In today's society, the reality of pagan gods still exist, although they are not labeled thusly. Anything that takes precedence or 1st place in our lives is our god. If we spend more time watching television than communing with God. If we devote more time seeking to fulfill our personal ambitions than fulfilling God's will for our lives; and even, if we endeavor to be the best church member, rather than seeking to be like Christ, we have still, unknowingly, fallen victim to this sin.

Let us begin and end each day with God being numero uno (No. 1) in our lives. Let us make His praise great and glorious as demonstrated through word and deed.

Day Two

*"Who is this who darkens counsel
by words without knowledge?"*
(Job 38:2)

We know God is loving, compassionate, forgiving, faithful, giving, and the list goes on, but the intrinsic knowledge and wisdom of God go beyond human comprehension. The above passage is God's introduction and opportunity for Job to answer questions that were impossible for him to even fathom.

Have you ever thought you knew the solution to a dilemma only to find out that you were nowhere close? As Christians, we often fall into this scenario. Because of our relationship with God, we begin to think that we understand how God thinks; or when we run into complications, we tell God how we want Him to fix them, and then we initiate the steps in doing so. The Bible teaches us differently. We are to trust God's omniscience (infinite knowledge). Being the Master Creator, God knows much better than we could ever comprehend how to 'fix' each one of our problems.

Taking matters in our own hands and then expecting God to clean up our mess is not faith or trust. However, we will find it to be a repeated action throughout biblical history with the Children of Israel. It is our own choice when we choose to do things our way, but we must also remember, consequences accompany our choices. God is forgiving and full of compassion but we must still reap what we've sown.

Day Three

*"Do not be afraid, Abram. I am your shield,
your exceedingly great reward—
And he believed in the Lord . . ."*
(Genesis 15:1 & 6)

Going into a covenant with God can bring about uncomfortable decisions and choices. The story of Abraham, who we often refer to as the Father of Faith, testifies to this truth.

A covenant differs from a promise in the sphere of response. A covenant is an agreement, which requires an act or action on behalf of those involved, but a promise is more of a pledge made by one. The most difficult challenge of going into a covenant with God is, although you may know the end result, you don't know the path you must travel to get there, nor the time involved.

God chose Abraham to be the father of many nations, but in order for him to receive this blessing, he would have to leave the comfort zone of his ancestral home and follow God's directions, although he had no idea of where he was going until he got there. That is called literally walking by faith.

Today, many of us have gone into a covenant relationship with God; we too have been given assignments and uncomfortable decisions and choices to make, but God reminds and encourages us, as He did Abraham, to trust Him and not be afraid; for He is our shield and protection; He is our great Rewarder. But we must trust and BELIEVE.

Day Four

*"This is the day the Lord has made;
we will rejoice and be glad in it."*
(Psalm 118:24)

Each day that the Lord allows us to see should be celebrated with praise and thanksgiving, for it is another opportunity to let our lights shine for kingdom building.

There are times when we tend to take the present for granted; putting off what God has called and empowered us to do today until tomorrow, forgetting that tomorrow is not promised to us. There are times when even those professing to be children of the Most High God tend to contract a case of convenient amnesia as it relates to remembering our purpose and assignment for the day. We often allow ourselves to become distracted with self-gratification and forget that our actions speak louder than our words. We mustn't forget that the manner in which we live our lives each day is a testimony of how we serve God. Although we might be able to eloquently quote Scriptures from the Bible, our true gratitude is shown in our attitude.

We have heard the saying, "People would rather see a sermon than hear one any day." Let us take this thought to heart— this day that the Lord has made.

Day Five

*"Thus also faith by itself, if it does
not have works, is dead."*
(James 2:17)

Work is a physical, as well as mental, effort or process. In the Epistle of James, we find there is a correlation between our faith and our work. Our action is truly a testimony of that which we believe.

A prime example of James' philosophy on faith can be found by reflecting over the lives of our fore-parents. Some have posed the question, "How did they do so much with so little?" I believe that the answer could be found in their efforts, which demonstrated faith in action. Although they didn't have very much, yet they offered unto God the best they had in time, talent and resources. And because of their faith, shown through their willingness to give, God answered their prayers with miracles.

Today we are indebted to those whose faith paved the way for us. I believe they are numbered in that great cloud of witnesses found in the 12th chapter of Hebrews, and I believe they are cheering us on. They have fought the good fight of faith; they have run their race; they have finished their course and passed the baton on to this generation. Will we accept our call to serve this present age, believing and trusting God to do what only God can do, or will we allow the cares of this world to smother out our torch and kill our faith? Let us remember, faith without works is dead.

Day Six

*"But God has chosen the foolish things
of the world to put to shame the wise—
that no flesh should glory in His presence."*
(1 Corinthians 1:27-29)

Education is crucial for our existence. The Bible is filled with instructions for us to teach others in order to reach others. The problem arises when one begins to focus more on academia and less on the guidance of the Holy Spirit. One can become so educated that he/she not only thinks, but believes that God has empowered him/her to know the thoughts of God. Even worse, one becomes so intellectually astute that he/she dares to declare and attempt to gain the support of others in the theory that there is no God; declaring the human race evolved from apes (evolution).

We are living in an age where accessibility to just about our every desire is finger-tip close. People don't have to leave the comfort of their homes to interact with the world around them. As Christians, we must not become hoodwinked by these fleshly perceptions and impressions. We will note, when studying God's Word, seldom we find the highly educated and sophisticated leaders bringing glory to God. In most cases, it is the least likely candidate, the ones whom man would have never chosen, that God chooses to bring glory to God. Why? — Could the answer be found in the above Scripture? So all would know that only by the grace and presence of God could such miracles happens.

Remember, as Christians, it is the Message, not the messenger that must be our focus.

Day Seven

"Trust in the Lord and do good"
(Psalm 37:3)

I fondly remember the words to a song that we often sang with fervor, when I was growing up, *"I'm gonna trust in the Lord 'til I die."* Although grammatically, the verses may have been considered somewhat Ebonics to the academically astute, I am of the belief that the essence behind the words was most pleasing to the heart of God.

God does work in a mysterious way. Reading Psalm 118:8, in which many believe is the center of the Bible, we find the words, "It is better to trust in the Lord than to put confidence in man." If we believe this to be true, then trusting God should be the Number 1 priority in our lives.

I encourage you this day to remember that God not only expects us to trust Him, but to also do good; for in due season we shall reap if we do not lose heart (Galatians 6:9).

WEEK SEVEN

Day One

"A man's gift makes room for him . . ."
(Proverbs 18:16)

A gift is a symbol of thoughtfulness. When we are blessed with a gift, regardless of how large or small, we can be assured of one thing— someone has been thinking about us. It's a good thing to be thought about in a positive manner; that's probably how the cliché, "It's the thought that counts" got started.

The Bible teaches God so loved us that He has given us gifts beyond measure and comprehension; the gift of His only Son, the gift of the Holy Spirit, and the gift of life, just to name a few. Each one of us has been given our own personal gift from God *(I Corinthians 7:7)*. To know we are thought of by our Creator should fill our hearts with gladness and joy. However; the observation today is not focused on the gift alone, but how we use it.

In the above Scripture we are told that our gifts make room for us; this means there is power in the gifts God has given, but there is a string attached — we must use them. An unused gift is of no value to anyone. God blesses us that we can be a blessing to others, but if we fall in love with the gift instead of the Giver, no growth can take place.

Do you desire to see God's power move miraculously in your life as well as the life of the Church? Begin really using the gifts God has given to you for God's glory. I think Paul says it best when he admonishes Timothy to "Stir up the gift of God" *(2 Timothy 1:6)*.

Day Two

*"But be doers of the Word, and not
hearers only, deceiving yourselves."*
(James 1:22)

Titles, positions and status are extremely sought after by some because of the implications and perceived power they hold. How others view us has a significant effect on our self-esteem; this is one reason many people try to fit in with the crowd or become a member of a clique.

On several occasions in my life, I can vividly remember people accusing me of losing my mind because of positions I chose to leave. One example would be resigning from what many viewed as a prestigious and lucrative position at a prominent television station to become a "common" school teacher. To this day, I'm often asked the question, "Why did you do that?" This type of thinking is not restricted to the secular world, for we have allowed it to seep into the Church.

Christians are followers of Christ; the path that we take may not be the one that would impress others, but it should be the ones God orders. The Bible teaches us that Jesus, the Son of God, who came to save us, was not held in high esteem. He was despised and rejected and became quite familiar with grief and sorrow *(Isaiah 53:3)*.

Let us ponder these questions: What level of Christian am I? Am I a Christian in name only, or am I a true follower of Christ? Am I a doer of God's Word or a hearer only?

Be not deceived, where there is no action, there is no faith.

Day Three

"This Book of the Law shall not depart from your mouth, but you shall meditate in it day and night ..."
(Joshua 1:8)

It is said we are living in the Joshua Generation, a time of passing the mantle of leadership to a new and younger group of people. Some call them non-traditionalists because they tend to think out of the box; some call them defiant because they refuse to keep doing the same thing the same way getting the same stagnant results. I call them spiritual change agents.

In the Book of Joshua, we find Moses' predecessor moving forward with God's ultimate plan of salvation; however, some of the people chosen to play major roles, and some of the tactics God used to bring to fruition a means to an end, would be considered ungodly and somewhat ludicrous by many staunch religious traditionalists. Joshua could have possessed this same type of thinking, but instead of buying into the earthly wisdom of people, he meditated and obeyed the Word of God.

Let us follow in Joshua's steps of trusting God's wisdom for the assignments we have been given. Let us focus on spending more time meditating and obeying God and less time trying to use our earthly wisdom to understand why God doesn't think like us; as the fact is, we should be trying to think to like God.

Day Four

"But without faith it is impossible to please Him (God), for he who comes to God must believe that He is, and that He is a rewarder of those who diligently seek Him."
(Hebrews 11:6)

If there was a recipe for **faith**, I believe it would call for: 1 cup of **courage**; 2 cups of **perseverance**, and 3 cups of **hope**.

Faith could not exist without courage, for courage is the opposite of fear; where there is fear, faith cannot abide. **Courage** gives us strength to persevere, or to keep on trying, regardless of the odds. I call **perseverance** courage's cheerleader. As we wait in confident expectation and anticipation (**hope**, not wishful thinking), we are empowered by the Holy Spirit to become witnesses of the miracles performed by the God of hope because of our belief in God revealed through our actions *(Romans 15:13)*.

Through many years of trials, tribulations and disappointments, I've found one thing to be steadfast — God's faithfulness to me. I dare not think it has been because of anything I've done to deserve it, but fully acknowledge it was only by God's grace and mercy. Since a youth, the Lord has been my hope and trust *(Psalm 71:5)*; my lifelong desire has been to please God; that's why I have had to learned how to walk by faith.

I invite you to join me today in this faith-walk. Let us together hold fast the confession of our hope without wavering; remembering, He who promised is faithful *(Hebrew 10:23)*.

Day Five

*"The Lord is good to those who wait for Him,
to the soul who seeks Him."*
(Lamentations 3:25)

There is an old adage that says, "Patience is a virtue." This tells me that the concept of waiting has been a struggle for a very long time— maybe even since the creation of humankind. In today's society, "waiting" appears to have become a thing of the past; not only do we not want to wait, in many instances we have become a wait-waivered people. For example, there was a time when children said they couldn't wait for their high school prom and graduation ceremony; well, in this 21st century, we can find children graduating as many as 3 times before they actually reach high school; there are some schools that offer middle school proms and even graduation rings.

The Bible has numerous Scriptures that focus on the importance of waiting. God cannot be compared to a superhero whose job is to come expeditiously to our every beckon call. God teaches us that "patience" must become a part of our spiritual nature if we are to grow and bear spiritual fruit *(Galatians 5:22).*

The above Scripture reassures us that good things do come to those who seek and wait on God. Let us discipline ourselves and our children in this concept. If God has promised us something, let us be patient and walk by faith, remembering and believing that He who promised is faithful and rewards those who diligently seek Him *(Hebrews 11:6).*

Day Six

*"Surely goodness and mercy shall follow me
all of the days of my life . . ."*
(Psalms 23:6)

The 23rd Psalm is one of the most popular psalms in the Bible. I believe we all can relate to King David's description of the Lord being our personal Shepherd; we all need someone to care for us as a shepherd cares for his flock, and no one can do this like Jesus.

In this Psalm, David tells us he is blessed because of the care he receives; and as he experiences the darkness of the valley, where death lurks and evil dwells, because his faithful Shepherd was with him every step of the way, he refused to give in to fear. Because of David's faith, he was allowed to witness God not only making a way for him, but showing him great favor.

As David ends this Psalm, he unapologetically states, that "surely" goodness and mercy would follow him all of the days of his life and he would dwell in the house of the Lord forever. These should be encouraging words for each one of us today as we experience the challenges this life offers.

Many of us are going through valley experiences right now. Some of us are even wrestling with the spirit of death (the loss of a loved one; the loss of a relationship; the loss of a job, etc.) Regardless of your challenge, remember you do have a Shepherd, One who cares for you in all situations and circumstances. Allow the Lord to order your steps and watch your life change. Once you realize that you're not going "through" alone, you will be able to see God move miraculously and become a witness to God's goodness and mercy chasing you, even in your valley experiences.

Day Seven

*"Let everything that has breath praise the Lord.
Praise the Lord!"*
(Psalm 150:6)

Are you breathing? Are you alive? If you answered yes to either question, here's one more — Are you praising the Lord?

No matter how tough life gets, we should always find time to praise God. Sometimes we feel as though we shouldn't have to go through some of the trials and hardships that God allows, but there is a reason. Our Father knows how easy it is for us to praise Him when things are in our favor, when the sun is shining bright and we don't have a care in the world. But God doesn't want, nor need, fair-weather children who give fair-weather praise. God wants us to know that He is the same God of yesterday, today and forever. It doesn't matter how our situation looks in the natural realm, we must remember God has ALL power and **is** in control.

Allow me to encourage you today, always praise God. Even if God doesn't do anything else for us, just think about what God has already done. That's more than enough reason to praise the Lord for the rest of our lives.

Let everything that has breath, praise the Lord!

WEEK EIGHT

Day One

*"How good and pleasant it is
when God's people live together in unity!"*
(Psalm 133:1—NIV)

*U*NITY is a small word with an extraordinary meaning. It is a sense of oneness. I have noted that when God's creation comes together on one accord, the sky is literally the limit.

There is a story found in Genesis 11:1-9 (*The Tower of Babel*), which attests to the power of oneness. Although in this story, the people united themselves for selfish and ambitious reasons, our focus should be on what they were able to accomplish by working together with the common goal being to build a tower so high that it would touch the heavens.

One of God's smallest creations, the ant, is another example of the power of oneness, in which unity is a key source for survival. When ants are on a mission, they remind me of soldiers. They appear to march in a synchronized line with one common objective; each one has a duty or responsibility to ensure the accomplishment of their mission. I have never witnessed one fighting with or trying to take over another's position. They seem to all know and accept their jobs.

There is a lesson to be learned from the ants, and even the fame-seeking tower builders, if they are and were able to unite and demonstrate the extraordinary power of oneness, how much more power do we, as followers of Jesus Christ, have when we live, work, and come together on one accord—putting God first?

Day Two

"—Do this in remembrance of Me."
(Luke 22:19)

Being brought up in the African Methodist Episcopal Church, I've always been exposed to the "open table" of the Lord's Supper. The significant transformation I can attest is the growth of understanding as to why it is done.

When I was a child, First Sundays were always a plus for me. Even though service was a little long, I could always look forward to the strange looking pieces of flat bread and tasty grape juice. As I grew into my upper teens, my desire to partake was not so great. By this time I had a better understanding of the concept. I must confess, there were a few Sundays I chose not to partake. We were taught by taking the Lord's Supper lightly (out of tradition or going through the motion), we would personally be responsible for bringing damnation to our souls. I wanted no part of that!

God does know our hearts and sees us in our secret places. Whether we put on a façade to blend in with the crowd, regardless of where the crowd may be, we are who we are; God knows and still loves us. The question we must answer individually is: Do we love God?

Jesus purposely instituted His Supper to remind us often about the great sacrifice He made for the sake of Love. Each time we partake of His table, let us make a new commitment to truly dedicate our lives to doing that which is pleasing in God's sight.

Day Three

"For I Am the Lord, I do not change"
(Malachi 3:6)

Seasons change and so do people. With each generation, it appears humankind becomes wiser with the wisdom of this world. This type of wisdom is foolishness in the eyes of the One who does not change *(1 Cor. 3:19)*.

As believers, we must always have an open heart and opened ears that we may be able to discern the voice of the Holy Spirit— seeking Godly wisdom should always be our aspiration for spiritual growth.

Socioeconomic status, educational degrees, and financial portfolios are all impressive to the carnal world, but not to God, for the Father is the Giver of every good and perfect gift *(James 1:17)*. If it is our desire to please God, then we must use that which we have been given for God's glory. This concept is nothing new, and God's expectations have not changed. The same God who created the heavens and earth, created you and me with a purpose in mind. We are spiritual change-agents and ambassadors for Christ *(2 Cor. 5:20)*. Our assignment is to introduce souls to the One who changes not, and Whose faithfulness, mercies and compassions are new each and every day *(Lamentations 3:22-23)*.

Day Four

"Then Jesus said to His disciples, 'If anyone desires to come after Me, let him deny himself and take up his cross, and follow Me.'"
(Matthew 16:24)

Bearing our cross can sometimes be similar to our view of going to heaven— everybody wants to go to heaven, but nobody wants to die.

Jesus plainly told His disciples that the only way we would be able to follow Him to that place where there are many mansions, the place in which Jesus went before us in preparation for our arrival, we must do two things: deny our own desires and take up our cross and do as Jesus did.

Most of us would want to enter into the pearly gates without the burdens of carrying our cross, but I have heard it put this way, "No Cross, No Crown." Crosses are meant to teach us, if we don't allow our circumstances to distract us from that which we should be learning. Crosses make us stronger and more aware of God's presence, power, and provisions.

If you are encountering a cross you feel is too heavy for you to bear, it probably is. Don't try to carry it by yourself, turn it over to Jesus and trust Him to do what you cannot, for His yoke is easy and His burdens are light *(Matthew 11:30)*. The presence of Christ is with you because He promised that He would never leave nor forsake us *(Hebrews 13:5)*; His power is omnipotent, there is nothing too hard for Him, and His provisions are plenteous, God is our Jehovah Jireh.

Day Five

*"Pride goes before destruction, and a
haughty spirit before a fall."*
(Proverbs 16:18)

*D*o you know anyone who always has to be right, or have the last word? Have you ever met someone who had the attitude of: *it's either my way or the highway?* You may have even crossed paths with someone who strongly disagreed with the majority's voice and since they couldn't convince others to think like them, instead of conceding to what was right in the game of life, they took their ball and went home.

These people, some our loved-ones and others our foes, have a strong sense of pride. In their minds, they cannot see pass their own way of thinking, whether right or wrong. They exist in the workplace, community, home and yes, even the church.

The above Scripture speaks of their fate, but the Message Bible translates it this way, "First pride, then the crash— the bigger the ego, the harder the fall."

If you know someone who thinks this way, or if these shoes could even fit your feet, remember; Power belongs to God *(Psalm 62:11).* And if God is on your side, you will always be in the majority, but you must put your trust and faith in your Father and not yourself.

The sin known as Pride is a dangerous spirit, it will take you where you don't want to go, keep you where you don't want to stay, and cost you more than you would ever want to pay.

Day Six

"The secret things belong to the Lord our God . . ."
(Deuteronomy 29:29)

*W*ho would have thought it?
Have you ever looked back on situations that seemed to be so illogical and found, maybe years later, something extraordinary was birthed out of them?

There are things that happen in our lives that we just can't fathom; they seem so irrational, but yet, God has a way of revealing His glory through un-thought-of means. I believe, in many instances, we can acknowledge these conditions, or strange happenings, as paths that lead to our destiny.

Believe it or not, God purposely allows some things to remain secret from us. In other words, there are things that we cannot explain, but deep in our hearts we must believe that they are somehow working together for our good.

I am reminded of the story of Moses. He was born during a time that all Hebrew male babies were being annihilated by command of Pharaoh, the Egyptian king *(Exodus 1-2)*. But God's infinite wisdom placed within the heart of Moses' mother an unorthodox means of saving her son from this death; God then orchestrated the unlikely possibility of Pharaoh's daughter adopting him. And as a testimony to God's amazing grace, a door was opened for Moses' own mother to become the Hebrew woman chosen to nurse him. The rest of the story—many years later, God used Moses to deliver the people of Israel out of the bondage of Egypt. Who would have thought it???

Day Seven

*"For as the body is one and has many members,
but all the members of that one body, being many
are one body, so also is Christ."*
(1 Corinthians 12:12)

*C*oming together on one accord and being at peace with each other could usher in the possibility of actually experiencing what it feels like to be one body with many members. Could it be that God used the example of unity and diversity in one body to help us understand just how much we truly need each other to survive? *(1 Cor.12:12-26)*

The most introverted person needs some human contact. Let us not find ourselves guilty of using the words that Cain used to answer God when asked about his brother, Abel *(Genesis 4:9)*. As children of the most-high God, we must remember we are our brothers and sisters' keepers.

If we are to survive as a country, a people, a family, and as members of the body of Christ, our actions must show that our words are from our hearts. The adversary's mission is to divide and conquer; however, remember Jesus said that a divided house cannot stand *(Mark 3:25)*.

If we don't stand for what is right, we will fall for what is wrong.

WEEK NINE

Day One

"—casting all your care upon Him, for He cares for you."
(1 Peter 5:7)

God cares for you.

Many times in life, defeating thoughts of failure will invade our minds if we are not careful. It is the enemy's job to send negative self-destructing messages to us through various means.

Derogatory statements are meant to hurt, not heal. You've heard people say: "He is too dark. She is too fat. She is too pale. He is too short. You're just like your mama. You're just like your daddy. She thinks she's better. He thinks he's smarter— etc."

Destructive criticism is just that— destructive. This problem usually comes from low self-esteem. Something is terribly wrong when the only way we can feel good about ourselves is when we are putting others down.

I challenge you this day; begin to cast out every negative thought that enters your mind. Give every hurt and pain you have had, or may be experiencing right now, to the One who cares so much that He gave His life so you might live. Be kind to those who revile, persecute, and say all kinds of evil things against you; we must not repay evil for evil, but God's Word tells us that if we see our enemy hungry, we should feed them; or if he is thirsty, we should get him a drink. Your generosity will surprise her with goodness. Don't let evil get the best of you; get the best of evil by doing good *(Romans 12:20-22 –Message)*.

God is a friend who cares for you, One who sticks closer than a brother *(Proverbs 18:24)*. And if we will humble ourselves in such a fashion, in due season, God will exalt us— because God does care for us *(1 Peter 5:6)*.

Day Two

*"To everything there is a season,
a time for every purpose under heaven."*
(Ecclesiastes 3:1)

One of the most difficult transitions that humankind must experience is change. It is a most challenging process to accept what we've seen for so long as the future evolving into the present; and what we've embraced for so long as the present making its way to the past. For such a bold statement, one would call for evidence to support this hypothesis. Traces of such support can be found in the behavior of parents who enable their children by refusing to allow them to grow up and become responsible and productive adults; or the young at hearts' monthly donations to products like Miss Clairol, Just for Men, and other anti-aging chemicals. And even in the church, there are those who attest to this change by refusing to release positions, and thought processes, for the good of the Church. Someone said the last seven words of a dying church are: "We've Never Done It That Way Before."

The Church Universal is in the transition of change. There is much talk about the Moses and Joshua Generations but until we learn how to embrace the good in both, we will not be able to see true productivity. Change will take place whether we accept it or not; I would equate it to childbirth for it is seldom easy, but hard labor. Our job is to believe that God has ordained a season for each one of us, and our prayer must be to serve to the best of our ability during our time; therefore, when change comes, we can rest in knowing that we can pass the torch to Joshua without hesitation, reservation, resentment or prejudice.

Day Three

> *"—He who is without sin among you,
> let him throw a stone . . . first."*
> (John 8:7)

*W*hy do we judge?
I posed this question to several people, young and young at heart, after the untimely death of a young man in Stanford, FL. The following answers were given: for power, control, status; lastly, a young adult told me that people judge because it's human nature. How would you answer this question?

The concept of judging is nothing new, as we will find it throughout the Bible. But how do we as Christians view it? In the chapter in which the above Scripture was taken, we find the religious leaders of Jesus' day attempting to trick Him into judging a woman's sin so that they could in return judge Him. Jesus knew their motives and instead of playing into their hands, He invited the ones who had no sin to cast the first stone.

It may be human nature to judge, but we should always remember, each of us has skeletons in our closets we would prefer to remain concealed. God has not called us to be judge or juror, but followers of Christ. Power, control, and status are all short lived if they are obtained in an ungodly manner. God will always have the last say.

If you know someone who is always judging others; remind them that God's Word says it is not our place to do so, and if we do, there is a consequence— we too will be judged by the same measure in which we judged others *(Matthew 7:1-2)*. Now, you without sin, cast the first stone.

Day Four

*"—work out your own salvation with fear and trembling;
for it is God who works in you both to will
and to do for His good pleasure."*
(Philippians 2:12-13)

We are familiar with the concept of work. It is basically a part of life for most people. We work to provide a livelihood for ourselves and families. The compensation from our labor empowers us to give our tithes, pay for our homes and automobiles, and buy necessities and luxuries for loved-ones. I believe we can agree that work is important.

Work is just as, and maybe even more, important in the spiritual realm. Jesus demonstrated this belief during His ministry on earth. He acknowledged the seriousness for Him to work while He could because there would come a time when work would not be an option *(John 9:4)*.

It is God who works in us to will and to do for His good pleasure (glory). Our time here on earth is really not about us, but about the assignments we have been given to complete. And it is of grave importance to know and remember — no assignment can be completed without WORK!

Some people live like they are never going to die, but there will come a day when night will come for each of us. God is not impressed with our socio-economic status, our homes, automobiles or bank accounts. God is impressed with our service to Him; how we treat each other; how we live our lives, and how we work out our gift of salvation.

When we work for God, God works through us!

Day Five

*"—I have no man to put me into the pool
when the water is stirred up . . ."*
(John 5:7)

*I*t has been said that, "excuses come a dime a dozen." If this is the case, we realize that excuses are probably the cheapest novelty on the market. I say novelty because they can be very innovative and creative. Children can really be ingenious when giving excuses as to why they didn't do their homework, or study for a test. But most of them get it honestly, for some parents can come up with unique excuses for their children, regardless of age.

We live in a world where excuses are a highly acceptable way of life. If you don't believe me, just talk to someone about why they don't go to church. In many instances, excuses have become habit.

The above scripture reveals the excuse a man, who had been crippled for 38 years, gives to Jesus when he was asked if he wanted to be healed. This man had been stationed by a healing pool for so long that when he started his new day, he had no idea he was next in line for a miracle, but God did. You see, this man had become so complacent with things being the way they were, he really had no hope of being healed— he was just going through the motions. Jesus did not have a long drawn out dialogue with the man, He simply said with authority, "Rise, take up your bed and walk."

Jesus knows our excuses, as he did the disabled man by the pool Bethesda, but He also wants to bless us in spite of them. It is time to put our excuses behind us. We can't change the past, but we sure can start a new day with a new attitude. Your miracle awaits!

Day Six

"Finally, brethren, whatever things are true, whatever things are noble, whatever things are just, whatever things are pure, whatever things are lovely, whatever things are of good report, if there is any virtue and if there is anything praiseworthy—meditate on these things."
(Philippians 4:8)

What's on Your Mind?

The United Negro College Fund slogan reminds us: "A Mind is a Terrible Thing to Waste."

Our minds are the tools we use to determine the type of existence we have here on earth. I would suggest that the mind is just as importance as the brain, for the brain is a valuable organ but God made the brain to think. By thinking even subconsciously, we know to breathe, eat, laugh, cry, and come out of the rain. All of our "know hows" are generated via the thinking process. In many, but not all, instances we determine to what degree of thinking we will do, for we must feed our brains, "Brain Food."

In his letter to the Church at Philippi, the Apostle Paul encourages the members to meditate, or think on a deeper level, about positive things; those concepts that would be pleasing to God. We do a lot of thinking, this is what the mind was made for, but the question is, "What are we thinking about?" Proverbs 23:7 declares, "as he (she) thinks in his (her) heart, so is he (she)." *(paraphrased)*

When we meditate on God's Word, we will be kept in perfect peace; God's peace surpasses all understanding.

Day Seven

"—Philip said to him, 'Come and see.'"
(John 1:46)

Have you ever been looking at television and out of the blue, you see someone you know? You become so excited that you call out to other family members or friends, "guess what, '*Michelle*' is on television, come and see."

Have you ever witnessed the first steps of a baby walking without holding on to the end table or someone's hand? You cry out: "*little John* is walking, hurry, come and see!"

Have you ever seen someone doing something that they should not have been doing— sneaking off from work; taking something that didn't belong to them, or maybe even abusing a loved-one or spouse? What was your response?

There is just something interesting about experiencing newness, or even disappointing encounters that make us want to tell others to "come and see."

This is how our walk with Jesus should be. We should always be ready to tell others about His grace and mercy in our lives; furthermore, we should be excited at the opportunity to share the "Good News". When we have found Jesus for ourselves, we should be like Philip and invite others to meet Him as well. There will always be skeptics like Nathanael (*John 1:46*), but it is not our responsibility to change their minds, Jesus can and will do this; but, we do have the power to encourage them to "come and see" for themselves.

WEEK TEN

Day One

"For as the heavens are higher than the earth,
So are My ways higher than your ways,
And My thoughts than your thoughts."
(Isaiah 55:9)

When things didn't go the way I thought they should go, my mother would kindly remind me that "God moves in mysterious ways." I didn't understand this adage until my faith-walk with Jesus began to grow stronger.

I think one of the most difficult challenges, for a Christian, involves accepting the fact that no matter how hard we try, we will never know the mind of God. During our life's journey, we experience some very difficult challenges; we lose loved-ones to death, divorce or the world; our physical bodies are attacked; our mental health becomes ill, and our friends turn against us. We try to figure out why a good God would allow these hurts and pains to enter into our lives. No one knows the mind of God; but during these times, God allows us the opportunity to affirm our relationship with the Son. If we accept Jesus' invitation and give Him our burdens *(Matt. 11:28-30)*, we will find, even though the happenings in our lives don't make sense, we can still walk in faith and find solace believing that somehow, God will bring great blessings out of them.

The Bible reveals the lives of many who came before us and encountered great challenges; however, they trusted God and were greatly rewarded for their faith. When your faith begins to falter, read the story of Joseph *(Genesis chapters 37 – 50)*; Daniel and his friends *(Daniel chapters 1 – 6)*, or the books of Job, Ruth and Esther, there you will find testimonies of God's mysterious ways.

Day Two

*"And whatever you do, do it heartily,
as to the Lord and not to men."*
(Colossians 3:23)

There are times in our homes, workplaces and churches, we witness others doing the minimum and receiving the more— more recognitions, more promotions, more wages, more entitlements, etc. This type of environment can cause apathy among those who try to live up to the expectations of the responsibility they have been afforded. Three stages usually take place: the first being in "disbelief" that superiors would actually allow these types of behaviors to exist without reprimand or correction; the second stage is that of "observation" — how long these minimum behaviors are permitted; and third stage is, "changes in behavior" — decreased performance because our efforts are being overlooked or not appreciated.

Equity is important in every facet of life, no one wants to be treated differently because of their ethnicity, gender or beliefs; however, we live in a world that is filled with prejudices.

I believe the above Scripture speaks to us today, as well as to the Church at Colosse, in whom Paul wrote. We live in an imperfect world, and unfortunately, we will probably witness or become a victim of inequity. It is in these times we must remind ourselves of Jesus' teachings about the world (John 14 – 16 chapters). Whatever the environment, our charge is to do the task with fervor, as if we were doing it for God.

In the words of my beloved grandmother, Jessie Mae Dedmon, *"All that you do, do with your might; things done half ain't ever done right!"*

Day Three

"Behold, I stand at the door and knock . . ."
(Revelation 3:20)

There was a time when the proper way to announce your presence at someone's house was by knocking on their door. Most times, if you were an expected guest, your knock was answered immediately with greetings of joy, however; when unexpected guests showed up, sometimes their greetings were less than hospitable. In some instances, the door never opened; inside the house could be heard the words: "Shhh— be quiet so they'll think we're not here and go away." Unfortunately, there have even been incidences when innocent children were taught the art of deception by their parents when instructed to respond: "Tell them we're not home."

The word "revelation" means to make known. In the biblical sense, it is a disclosure of a divine truth and will to humankind. In the above passage it is understood that Christ is revealing the condition of the Church at Laodicea. Although they were economically well-off, He described their works for Him as lukewarm (neither hot nor cold). In word they professed to be the Church of Christ, but it appeared He had actually become an uninvited guest in His own House; therefore, He stood at the door and knocked, awaiting their invitation to enter.

In today's society, many have been blessed with all manner of wealth, but we must not allow these earthly riches to leave us spiritually impoverished; we mustn't forget the Giver. Let us not forget that in order to be available vessels for Christ, we must first open the doors of our hearts and let Him in. Behold, He stands knocking.

Day Four

"Blessed is He who comes in the name of the Lord!
The King of Israel!"
(John 12:13)

While attending a FLAME (Faithful Leaders As Mission Evangelists) Conference at St. Simmons Island, GA, a few years back, we were introduced to a song the conference leaders were adamant about us learning; it was entitled, "Everybody Ought to Know Who Jesus Is." We sang this song everyday and were encouraged to even create and add new verses. Their global theme was, "That the World May Know Jesus Christ."

In the above Scripture, we find Christ, just a few days away from His crucifixion, being acknowledged as the King of Israel; the Savior of the world. He had ridden into town sitting on the back of a young donkey in fulfillment of the prophecy found in Zachariah 9:9, which proclaimed that the Messiah would be revealed symbolically in this manner. And just for a brief time in history, the people knew who Jesus was. They honored His Lordship by placing their clothing and leafy branches on the ground upon which He trod, and they went out to meet Him waving their palm branches and crying out: "Hosanna!" During this Triumphal Entry, they honored Him, but just a few days later— rejection came.

Let this memory speak to our spirits. Let us pray that we don't become Palm Sunday Christians only. And let us not forget who Jesus really is and what He really did to save us from our sins.

Day Five

"Also I heard the voice of the Lord, saying: 'Whom shall I send, and who will go for Us?' Then I said, 'Here am I! Send me.' And He said, 'Go and tell this people . . .'"
(Isaiah 6:8-9)

"Connect, Act, Respond and Experience" was one of the quadrennial themes of the Women's Missionary Society of the A.M.E. Church.

I found these words both fitting and crucial for such a group of people whose purpose is to serve. Each word is an action verb which reminds us that the role of a missionary is to perform a task.

There is much work to be done in our communities, but the rhetorical question which continues to arise is, "Who will do it?" Let us step out of our comfort zones and view the real world of hurting people who need our help. There are those who need someone to tell them about the God who is able to heal every pain; the God who will supply their every need; the God who loves them so much that He gave this world the very best He had in His Son, Jesus, to save us from the bondage of sin. Not only must we tell them, but we must show them by allowing them to experience God's love through our actions.

We are all missionaries. If we say we are followers of Christ, our actions should always say the same. God's will is the same today as it was in the day of Isaiah; He still bids us to "Go and tell this people."

Day Six

"—knowing that the testing of your faith produces patience. But let patience have its perfect work . . ."
(James 1:3-4)

The butterfly is one of the most beautiful and fascinating creations of God. Beautiful because its appearance varies in style, size, color, and design; fascinating because of the way it transforms into its beauty. As a child, I often wondered how something so beautiful could evolve from such a creepy "worm-like" bug. But God! Only God could have seen passed the exterior appearance to visualize the beauty that hibernated within.

Many times in life we see so much potential (beauty) in people; however, often they can't see it in themselves. We try to encourage them; we pray for them, and even, unknowingly, enabled them. Finally we realize all of our efforts are in vain, for until they face their season of transformation, nothing we do will make them change. They must go through their metamorphosis on their own. This is where patience on our behalf is crucial. It is only when we allow them the opportunity to grow without our help, and start believing that God can and will transform their lives, that faith steps up and insists that we wait for God to bring it to pass.

If you are struggling with seeing the transformation of a loved-one, I encourage you to let patience have its perfect work. It might take longer than you'd like, but don't give up on them. Something beautiful will emerge.

Day Seven

"Then Jesus, looking at him, loved him, and said to him, 'One thing you lack: Go your way, sell whatever you have and give to the poor, and you will have treasure in heaven; and come, take up the cross, and follow Me.'"
(Mark 10:21)

*A*re you living your heaven here on earth? God wants us to enjoy life, that's why we are afforded the opportunity to experience wonderful things. Whether financial stability, family, and/or good health; they are all blessings from God. We say, "Life is good" when things are going our way, but when the burden of a cross summons our attention, we often forget that life in Christ is still good.

Burdens have a way of stealing our joy because we have to take up crosses we didn't ask to carry. It is in these times we should reflect on another familiar saying, "No cross, no crown." There are some good-hearted people in this world; I have had the privilege of meeting those who would give you the shirt off their backs. Many don't even profess to be Christian, but have commendable qualities. There's only one problem. God did not call us to be "good," but "righteous."

In the 10th chapter of Mark, we find a story about a rich young ruler; he was a good person who followed of the commandments of God. One day he came running to Jesus asking what he should do to inherit eternal life when his earthly days were over; Jesus lovingly told him the way, but the young man couldn't bear the cross of parting with his earthly possessions. He was crushed and walked away in the spirit of sadness. Although he followed the law, he was not willing to follow Jesus. Let us be reminded that this world is not our home; the treasures we obtain here are temporal, but the kingdom of God is eternal.

WEEK ELEVEN

Day One

"—And try Me now . . . Says the LORD of hosts,
If I will not open for you the windows of heaven
And pour out for you such blessing . . ."
(Malachi 3:10)

Consciously, no man or woman would ever think about robbing God; yet, the 8th verse of the third chapter of Malachi begins with a hard-pressed question, "Will a man rob God?" And it is followed by an accusation.

God explains through the Prophet Malachi that His people rob Him when they do not give back a portion of that which He has freely given them— their tithes and offerings. And for those who were a little leery of following God's command (as though it may have been a bad investment), God encouraged them to "try" Him by stepping out in faith. God promised for their faithfulness, He would open up the windows of heaven and pour out so many blessings that there would not be room enough to receive them all.

There is also another side to this commandment found in the New Testament. In the 5th chapter of Acts, you will find a story about a married couple by the names of Ananias and Sapphira, who not only lied to the Apostles about their giving, but also to the Holy Spirit. God punished both by striking them dead.

Some may say that God does not have the same expectations for His people today as He did during biblical times, but God does not change *(Malachi 3:6)*. God does not want our excuses; God desires our submission to His will. If you have not already, I encourage you to accept God's challenge and "try" God for yourself.

Day Two

*"Oh, taste and see that the Lord is good;
blessed is the man who trusts in Him."*
(Psalm 34:8)

Can we judge a book by its cover? How will we know if the fruit is really sweet? How can we attest to the Lord's goodness? The answer to each of these questions is one in the same— we must personally partake. The book, we must read. The sweetness of the fruit must be confirmed by one of our five senses. And the Lord's goodness, we must experience.

The 34th Psalm is one of my favorites psalms because it blesses God in spite of present situations and circumstances. King David learned to trust God in the good times, as well as those engulfed in challenges. Once he tasted (experienced) God's grace and mercy, David believed God would bless him even in the midst of his storms, and God did just that.

Have you tasted God's goodness in your life? I have. That's why I can and do bless the Lord, even in the worst of times, His praises are continually in my mouth. I dare not tell God about how big the mountains are in my life; instead I tell the mountains that I serve an awesome God who is large and in charge; One who specializes in transforming mountains into molehills.

Day Three

*"—Render therefore to Caesar the things that are
Caesar's and to God the things that are God's."*
(Matthew 22:21)

*D*aily, we are faced with tests. One of the most difficult tests some encounter is that of giving, or sacrifice. Our reluctance comes from an attitude of self-assurance. This attitude implies that we have a selective methodology in which we choose to trust God. In many instances, this attitude signifies where our true allegiance lies. Jesus said that where your treasure is, there your heart will be also *(Matt. 6:21)*. Everything we have is a gift from God. As citizens, we have the civic responsibility to pay our taxes, and we do; but what about our godly responsibilities? Do we render "the things" of God back to God? Time, talent, resources and money are all given by our Father. How do we thank Him? If we really believe that the Father is the Giver of every good and perfect gift *(James 1:17)*, our lives should exemplify this trust. We mustn't make the mistake of putting anything or anybody before God in our lives. We are God's children, grafted into His family by the precious blood of Jesus.

The next time you are faced with the test of giving, take a few minutes to remember that "God so loved the world (this includes you) that He gave His only begotten Son (Jesus), that whosoever believes in Him should not perish (go to hell), but have everlasting life" *(John 3:16)*. What more is there to say?

Day Four

*"Now faith is the substance of things hoped for,
the evidence of things not seen."*
(Hebrews 11:1)

*I*n the arena of Christianity, we are reminded our whole earthly journey is one of faith. "So just what is this 'faith' word?" some may ask. The answer lies in our true belief in the realness of God.

For many, faith has its proper place in the box of perception. People who are working toward a goal, with knowledge of the end results, fit into this category. For example, one who has never driven to Denver, CO, but decides to head out with the help of a road map. Even though this person may take the wrong turn here and there, because of the tool being used, the likelihood of him getting back on the right road and making it to his destination is good.

As Christians, we too have a map, better known as a Guide who helps us while we're on our earthly journey, God the Holy Spirit. The tool that navigates us through life is called the Bible. The difference is, our directions are all abstract; we cannot see the outcome; we are not sure of what lies ahead, but we are convinced of the reality of God, and we trust the Holy Spirit to order our steps. Those who do not walk in faith cannot see past the physical world in which they live; but those who walk in faith are open to the spiritual realities of God.

God rewards those who diligently seek Him in faith and without faith, it is impossible to please God *(Hebrews 11:6)*.

Day Five

"And do not be conformed to this world, but be transformed by the renewing of your mind . . ."
(Romans 12:2)

I often think of how God uses the term sheep to describe us. When I think about the characteristics of sheep, one perception sticks out the most— they were never meant to exist on their own, but to be guided by their shepherd. Because of their shepherds, sheep make contributions to the world by sacrificing their wool for manufacturing purposes. But if they were left on their own, these contributions would not exist, for sheep do not have the mindset to present themselves to the shear; furthermore, without the shepherd's guidance, they could find themselves roaming in wolves' territory.

Because of our human nature, oftentimes it is much easier for us to distance ourselves from our Shepherd by wandering into the unknown territories of life. We see others take these paths and tend to conform to their mindsets and theologies because little sacrifice is required and it's comfortable. This is not God's will for our lives. As Christians, sheep of the true and Good Shepherd *(John 10:11)*, it is our duty to follow and be guided by Christ. If we allow Jesus to lead us, our minds will be transformed; we won't mind sacrificing for His namesake, and we will walk in the path of righteousness all of the days of our lives.

Day Six

"—So he began to speak boldly in the synagogue. When Aquila and Priscilla heard him, they took him aside and explained to him the way of God more accurately."
(Acts 18:26)

God desires more team players. No man or woman is an island. The Bible tells us that two is better than one *(Ecclesiastes 4:9-12)*.

Apollos was a very intelligent man. We are told he was an eloquent and fervent speaker for God, who knew the Scriptures *(Acts 18:24-25)*. He knew a lot, but not enough. One day Apollos was boldly teaching in Corinth, when Aquila and Priscilla (husband and wife) heard him. This couple had spent some time with the Apostle Paul and knew quite a bit about the teachings and resurrection of Christ. It was in Aquila and Pricilla's hearts to help Apollos become even more successful in teaching God's way, so in an effort to assist, they privately taught him the things he needed to know for his ministry and the glory of God.

We can learn much from this biblical demonstration of team work, but two important factors are: 1) Aquila and Pricilla's desire was to help and not hurt. They could have easily allowed the spirit of jealousy to enter into their hearts to criticize Apollos' lack of knowledge. 2) Apollos had a willing heart to accept the information they had to share for the glory of God. He could have easily rejected the knowledge they offered, as they were tent makers, not scholars.

Team work is important in our families, on our jobs and in our churches. The produce of our labor is so much greater when we all work together toward a common cause.

Day Seven

"—in the last days perilous times will come"
(II Timothy 3:1)

We live in a world filled with various means of technological communication. We have the various smart phones, pagers, emails, text messaging, internet, news media, facebook, twitter, instagram, devices in our automobiles, and GPS systems, just to name a few. We find ourselves constantly competing with something that demands or takes our attention away from what we could, or should be doing; what we should be learning, and what we should be hearing. These, sometimes extraneous variables, could be labeled as distractions: for when our attention is on them, we lose connection with that which our minds were on originally.

Technology can be a very helpful tool, but we should make it work for us without losing our souls to it.

A few years ago I met a very nice family oriented lady who was introduced to the wiles of the web. She met a guy on a site who literally blew her mind. She ended up leaving what she had professed to be her happy Christian home (husband and children), and moved to another state to be with her new found internet love. I realize this story seems a little far-fetched, but it really did happen.

Technology is not evil, but it is an avenue for those who are gullible and lonely to be lured into perilous territory. Every thing should be done in moderation; for when something captures our time and attention more than God, we'll find ourselves, unknowingly, slaves to it. How much time are you devoting to technology?

WEEK TWELVE

Day One

*"But the manifestation of the Spirit is
given to each one for the profit of all."*
(1 Corinthians 12:7)

Somewhere in history, division was afforded the opportunity to breed into the lives of God's people by means of diversity. We have allowed our differences to dictate how we view ourselves, as well as how we view others. In many ways, we have become more self-serving.

Somehow, we have allowed the adversary to bamboozle us into believing that the choices we make are of no consequence to others, but this is the farthest deception from the truth.

It is not by coincidence that you are where you are during this season of your life. The Holy Spirit has ordained you with a special gift (an ingredient) needed to bring to fruition that which has been purposed for God's good for such a time as this. The Apostle Paul puts it in elementary terms for an inclusive understanding. He symbolically uses the human body to make his point, for every part of our body is vital for us to function properly; no matter how large or small, each one has its own job and is expected to do its part for the profit of all. When just one part fails to work properly, the whole body suffers.

God expects us to use what we've been given for the edification of the Church; we must use our gifts for the glory of God, for we are the body of Christ *(1 Cor. 12:27)*.

Day Two

"Death and life are in the power of the tongue—"
(Proverbs 18:21)

So many times, we unknowingly curse ourselves with our own words. We speak in the negative. We boldly say what we cannot do. We may even see ourselves as "grasshoppers," unable to achieve the challenges set before us because we view them as giants *(Numbers 13:33)*, not opportunities.

It is time for us to stop allowing the enemy to feed us lies. We must begin seeing with spiritual eyes, hearing with spiritual ears, and speaking with words of hope and life.

If only we understood the power of our tongue. Do you realize when we say we can't, we "loose" the power of failure against us *(Matt. 16:19)*; and we become our own worst enemy, ensuring defeat. How can we sing that our hope is built on Jesus' blood and righteousness in one breath, and speak words of gloom, doom and despair in the next? Is our hope in the power of God or ourselves? God didn't call us to be successful, but to be faithful. We must leave the success of our efforts in the hands the Lord.

There is an urgency to disband all of the "can'ts" in your vocabulary, and replace them with "cans." Begin to see yourself and others as victors, not victims. Speak words of life over your family; speak words of life over your community, and speak words of life over your church. Remember, you "**CAN**" <u>do all things</u> **through Christ who strengthens you** *(Phil. 4:13)*.

Day Three

"Do not forget to entertain strangers, for by so doing some have unwittingly entertained angels."
(Hebrews 13:2)

*D*o you believe in angels? The Bible speaks of them from Genesis (16:7) to Revelations (12:16). I believe angels dwell among us, seen and unseen. This poses a somewhat awkward question: Have you ever entertained one?

The writer of Hebrews tells us to be careful as to how we entertain strangers, because we never know just who they may be. But there is one thing for certain, if God sends them to cross our path, there is a reason, and how we respond is of the utmost importance.

From this day forth, I challenge you to treat everyone who crosses your path as though they were angels of God; by doing so, we will not only be obedient to the Scriptures, but also become more aware of our actions toward others. Remember, the first and great commandment is to love the Lord our God with ALL of our hearts, souls, and minds, but the second is like it: "You shall love your neighbor as yourself" *(Matthew 22: 36-39).*

Day Four

"I, the Lord, search the heart, I test the mind, even to give every man according to his ways, according to the fruit of his doings."
(Jeremiah 17:10)

The Bible says: *as one thinks in his heart, so is he (Proverbs 23:7a).*

This revelation inspires and encourages us to be careful of the thoughts that we entertain. Thoughts are the seeds of our actions, and the adversary feeds on our weaknesses. What makes it so credulous, he comes at us the same way every time, but because our thinking is not clear, we usually don't see him coming until it is too late.

God searches our hearts. God knows what we think, how we feel, and our hearts' desires. It is God's desire to fulfill each one of ours, but we must be ready to accept His divine interventions. God doesn't do things the way we "think" God should, for God's thoughts and ways differ from ours as much as the heavens are higher than the earth *(Isaiah 55:9)*. In spite of our shortcomings, God still loves us; and He tests us to see if we are able to receive the blessings He has purposed for our lives. If our hearts are not right, God has to withhold our precious gifts until we are ready to receive them.

How is your mind today? What thoughts are you thinking? Are they pleasing to God, or are they focused more on the world's way of doing things? Remember, God is checking us out and giving to each one of us according to our ways.

Day Five

*"He counts the number of the stars;
He calls them all by name."*
(Psalm 147:4)

*W*hat an awesome God we serve! Can you comprehend the ability to not only count the stars, but call each one by their given name? I can't. Sometimes I get my three children's names mixed up and call one by the other's — some call it a senior moment, and that may be true, but I call it being human.

Just as God created, named, and numbered the stars, God has an even greater creation — you and I (humankind). King David proclaims God formed him while he was yet in his mother's womb and made him "fearfully and wonderfully" *(Psalm 139:14)*. In other words, God made him "an awesome wonder." We too must understand just how precious we are to our Creator. Believe it or not, God knows each one of us by name, and has created us for greatness.

Have you ever taken the time to really gaze upon the twinkling of the stars? Have you seen the formations they make? Can you attest to their beauty? If you can answer 'yes' to any one of these questions, then you must understand that God created us to outshine the stars. God has equipped us with everything we need; now all we have to do is use it.

Lest we forget that God called us out of darkness into His marvelous light so we too could shine. We are a chosen generation, a royal priesthood, a holy nation; God's own special people *(1 Peter 2:9)*. Let us proclaim God's praise to everyone we meet, and let our actions be those of believers.

Day Six

"And you will seek Me and find Me,
When you search for Me with all your heart."
(Jeremiah 29:13)

A few years ago, author Tommy Tenney wrote a book entitled, "The God Chasers." Its focus is on those who actually have a perpetual desire or spiritual hunger and thirst to stay in the presence of the Lord; therefore, one's life is spent seeking God. God chasers are different from the average Christian. They not only come to church on Sunday, but you will also find them seeking God and God's will for their lives every day. No decision is made without consulting the Master first. Some might even call them "spiritual addicts," for their lives are dedicated to seeking and serving God; with the ultimate purpose of bringing glory to God and edification to God's kingdom here on earth.

King David says that his greatest desire was to always be near the presence of God *(Psalm 27:4)*. Sometimes this desire led David to places that were out of his comfort zone, but he trusted God to deliver him from all of his fears, and God did *(Psalm 34:4)*.

I praise God for my mother's intuition. She felt the need to share with me my desire to seek God even as a two-year old. After giving birth to my brother, while she was still incapacitated, a neighbor cried out from across the street early one Sunday morning; she had spotted me in the middle of the gravel road crawling to the church house about a block from where we lived.

Are you a God Seeker? God says, when you search for Him with all of your heart, you will find Him.

Day Seven

"O God, You are my God; early will I seek You . . .
When I remember you on my bed, I meditate on You
in the night watches . . . My soul follows close behind You;
Your right hand upholds me."
(Psalm 63:1; 6 & 8)

*R*elationships are vital for healthy living, mentally, socially, physically, and spiritually, for our Creator deemed it so.

Recall the words found in Genesis 2:18, "And the Lord God said, 'It is not good that man should be alone; I will make him a helper comparable to him.'" God wants us to have wonderful relationships with our spouses, parents, children, siblings, and friends, but God also desires us to have a relationship with Him.

Knowing about God is a good thing, but to know God is much, much better. I believe this is one of the reasons there has been such a decline in overall church attendance during the past twenty years. People don't understand to obey God's "First and Great Commandment" (to love God with all of our hearts, souls and minds – *Matt. 22:37-38*), means to establish a love relationship with God, even greater than our earthly ones.

Our challenge in this 21st century is to not only introduce our brothers and sisters to Jesus, but to teach them the importance of establishing a relationship with Him through our testimonies. The Word says, "Faith comes by hearing and hearing by the Word of God." *(Romans 10:17)*.

I personally agree with Kirk Whalum and Jonathon Butler, falling in love with Jesus is the best thing I've ever done, and this my soul knows well!

THE LITURGICAL CALENDAR & HOLIDAYS

New Year's Day

"Death and life are in the power of the tongue . . ."
(Proverbs 18:21)

How careful we must be of the words we allow to flow from our lips.

"Choose your words wisely." Have you ever really thought about the meaning of this phrase? How many times have you uttered out words that within seconds you wished you had kept to yourself, or said differently? Words are powerful and the tongue can be ever so vicious if it is not controlled *(James 1:26; 3:8)*.

As we begin this New Year, let us remember "Life" and "Death" are in the power of the tongue. Did you know that through faith, God has given us the power to speak life into every situation that confronts us? It was because of Abraham's faith in God he became the father of many nations *(Romans 4:17-20)*.

Let us begin and end this year with a "can do" spirit and attitude. Let us speak life into our hopes, dreams, and desires. And let us remember that our God is able to do exceedingly abundantly above ALL that we ask or think, according to the power that works in us *(Ephesians 3:20)*.

In the mighty name of Jesus, I speak the spirit of peace, love, and joy into the lives of each family of the one reading this devotion. Into your lives, I speak the spirit of kindness, goodness, faithfulness, gentleness, and self-control. And into your lives, I speak the spirit of prosperity; calling and believing God to meet every need, every hope, and every desire of your hearts *(Mark 11:23)*. By the power of the Holy Spirit, we receive it as already done. AMEN

Dr. Martin Luther King, Jr. Day

"I will not leave you orphans; I will come to you."
(John 14:18)

*D*o you view being difference as a negative, positive, or neutral stance? For many, the word "different" carries a negative connotation. People who don't fit into what we view as the "norm" are often labeled as "different." In many instances, being different sets people apart; causes exclusions, and sometimes produces the spirit of prejudice. The truth of the matter is, being different can produce feelings of loneliness and despair, but we must remember, we are never alone, for God is with us.

Jesus was well acquainted with sorrow, grief and loneliness, but He knew regardless of how things looked or felt, His Father was faithful and would not abandon Him.

Today marks the birthday of the Reverend Dr. Martin Luther King, Jr., one who was considered different during his day because he not only dared to dream, but was bold enough to speak his dreams aloud. Although, it may have been because of his stance to speak out in protest of the racial inequality he was slain, today we are able to reap many benefits from his efforts and sacrifice.

Remember, the Bible tells us that we (followers of Christ) are a peculiar people *(1 Peter 2:9 – KJV)*. So if being different in the eyes of others make us special in the eyes of God— so be it.

February — Black History

"I would have lost heart, unless I had believed . . ."
(Psalm 27:13)

This is the month in which we set aside to acknowledge the history; emphasize the accomplishments, and affirm the contributions of a people who evolved from slavery to productive citizens in these United States. This is also the month in which we celebrate the first black organized institution in the United States, the African Methodist Episcopal Church (1816).

On February 14, 1760, Richard Allen was born. It was because of the efforts of this former Delaware slave and others, this denomination was birthed. He was elected and consecrated the 1st Bishop of this historic Church.

Think about what it must have taken for a group of people, who were viewed as second-class citizens, to organize and institute such a feat during a time when the odds were stacked up highly against them. How could they do it? I would surmise they called upon the One in whom they put their trust and **believed** to be faithful and true.

When the odds are against you, it is easy to lose heart if we don't have an anchor, but we do. Our faith and trust are anchored and grip the Solid Rock, Jesus, who continues to tell us, as He told our fathers and mothers of all faiths, "If you can **believe**, all things are possible to him (those) who believes." *(Mark 9:23)*

Valentine's Day

*"For God so loved the world that He gave
His only begotten Son . . ."*
(John 3:16)

John 3:16 is probably one of the most quoted and remembered Scriptures found in the New Testament. The foundation of our existence and hope of our salvation are founded on four little letters: L-O-V-E.

This Scripture, alone, reminds us no matter how discouraging things may appear, because of God's love for us, and the awesome sacrifice of His precious One and only Son, Jesus Christ; we have the confidence in knowing that everything will work out for the good.

We all have valley experiences, but as we walk through, let us be reminded we are not alone, for God the Son loved us so much that He promised never to leave nor forsake us. And He was so committed to His word that He gave His life so we would not lose ours. "Greater love has no one than this, than to lay down one's life for his friends" *(John 15:13)*. Jesus also commanded us, His followers, to **love** one another *(John 15:17)*.

Today, as you commune with special loved-ones in your life, don't forget to spend some time with the One who is LOVE *(1 John 4:8)*.

The more love you give away, the more love you have! Happy Valentine's Day!

FOR GOD
    SO LO**V**ED THE WORLD
      TH**A**T HE GAVE HIS
    ON**L**Y
  BEGOTT**E**N
    SO**N** SO
    THA**T** WHOEVER
   BEL**I**EVES
     I**N** HIM SHALL
  HAV**E** EVERLASTING
          LIFE

Ash Wednesday

"For Christ also suffered once for our sins, the just for the unjust, that He may bring us to God . . ."
(1 Peter 3:18)

Ash Wednesday signifies the beginning of the forty days (excluding Sundays) of Lent; these forty days represent the time in which Jesus spent in the wilderness, wherein all three synoptic Gospels attest to His purpose of fasting and praying, and lastly being tempted by satan.

Lent is one of the oldest observances on the Christian calendar and its purpose has been to set aside a time of personal reflection, prayer, fasting, almsgiving, and penitence (repentance), demonstrated by self-denial in preparation for the Easter celebration.

The above Scripture reminds us Jesus gave up His life so we might be reconciled to God our Father. This Lenten season, I pray each of us will take a serious look back over our lives and acknowledge the blessings we've encountered because of God's love, grace, mercy and goodness. Remember, God the Father so loved us that He gave His Son *(John 3:16),* and Christ the Son loved us so much that He gave His life *(John 10:15).* Let us ask ourselves, "What am I willing to give up for God?"

First Day of Lent

*"—For all things come from You,
And of Your own we have given You."*
(1 Chronicles 29:14)

During this season of Lent, we purposely give up something that we will greatly miss in remembrance of the great sacrifice Jesus made on our behalf. Let us remember that regardless of what we have— be it power, honor, strength, or wealth, they all came from God.

King David made a magnanimous and bold gesture because of his love for God. Not only did he give over and above out of his own special treasure, he encouraged others to consecrate themselves to the Lord. David knew those who were willing to consecrate themselves to the Lord, would have no difficulty in willingly giving back to Him what He had given them, because their hearts were loyal to God.

If you have not yet consecrated yourself to the Lord, you have been given another opportunity to do so today. You will find that it won't be difficult to give up something that means a lot to you during this season, or the seasons to come. Trust God to take that which you freely give and multiply it a hundredfold back to you. Remember, every good gift and every perfect gift comes from God *(James 1:17)*, so you're actually just giving back a portion to God of that which God first gave to you.

Palm Sunday

"—they . . . took branches of palm trees and went out to meet Him, and cried out: Hosanna! Blessed is He who comes in the name of the Lord! The King of Israel!"
(John 12:12-13)

Today we celebrate Palm Sunday, the day in which Jesus made His Triumphant Entry into Jerusalem on the back of a young donkey — the day in which the crowd met Him with palms and acknowledged Him as the King of Israel. Yes, but also the day that plots to kill Him began to thicken and the culmination of His coming would be manifested to all humankind.

This should be a very thought-provoking week for Christians, the week in which we've labeled, "Holy." It is my prayer we will walk each day with Jesus during His last days. Let us prepare our hearts for the great sacrifice of love that was poured out for us. Will we love those who praise us today and turn their backs on us by Friday? Will we wash the feet of those who will carry the burden of the cross after our departure? Will we go to the Garden of Gethsemane praying with the agony of knowing our time has come to face the reason for which we came? Will we go to the Cross with Jesus?

Jesus said, "Whoever does not bear his cross and come after Me cannot be My disciple." *(Luke 14:27)*

I pray this week will help us to remember there is a cross for each of us— and it's up to us to carry it; knowing we are following the One who carried our sins to Golgotha, where He was crucified for our sakes.

Easter Day

"—Do not be afraid. Go and tell . . ."
(Matthew 28:10)

$\mathcal{A}$re you fearful of witnessing to others God's plan of salvation? Does it make you uncomfortable to invite those who don't know Jesus to church? Do you keep all of the wonderful miracles God has performed in your life a secret because you're afraid of what others may say or think about you? Your answers will reveal your faithfulness and obedience to God's Word.

Fear is a detrimental weapon the adversary uses against us. Jesus left with us the Great Commission of spreading the Good News of His life, death, and resurrection, but if satan can plant seeds of fear into our spirits, we will tend to coward down to the charge we have been given. We know that the spirit of *fear* is not given by God *(2 Timothy 1:7)*; so when it attempts to make its abode with us, we must learn to combat it with faith.

As we celebrate this blessed Easter Day, let us remember Christ's instructions given to the women, who were the first witnesses of His resurrection. They were told, "Do not be afraid," then "Go and tell." The last Words in the 28th Chapter of Matthew reveals Jesus' commissioning His disciples to go into all the world, baptizing and teaching God's plan of salvation; however, with this commission Jesus made a promise. Christians in the 21st century should understand that this promise is as applicable today as it was when Christ said, **"And lo, I AM with you always, even to the end of the age."**

Mother's Day

*"—O woman, great is your faith!
Let it be done to you as you desire."*
(Matthew 15:28)

Growing up in rural Arkansas, there was a saying that described mothers who had a strong commitment to their children, or the children whom God had placed under their care: "She's just like a mother hen." Since my parents raised chickens, I was blessed with the opportunity to observe them on a daily basis. As I grew older, I came to understand the significance of this saying. If you don't know very much about chickens, allow me to enlighten you. Hens are very docile creatures, scary by nature; they usually stay away from humans except at feeding times, but when hens have chicks, their personality changes. The fear that once kept them clear of humans is replaced with a courageous love for their biddies (baby chicks). And the wise human knows unless there is a desire to get pecked, it is better to stay clear of the mother hen.

In the above Scripture, we find a woman whose actions could be compared to that of a mother hen's. Under normal circumstances, instead of approaching Jesus, I'm sure she would have been steering clear, as her culture would denote; but her love for her child made it necessary to persevere in spite of the possible consequences.

Like the hen, a mother's love is uncompromising. It is only superseded by the love of God through Jesus Christ, who, Himself, acknowledges the hen's commitment to protect her chicks *(Matt. 23:37)*. Every day is a great day to honor mothers!

Pentecost Sunday

*"When the Day of Pentecost had fully come,
they were all with one accord in one place . . ."*
(Acts 2:1)

Today, we celebrate the special day promised by our Lord and Savior, Jesus the Christ; the day that the Holy Spirit descended and gave power to His followers.

We know the Holy Spirit is the third Person of the Godhead (Trinity), but to some, that is as far as our knowledge goes. The Holy Spirit is God who lives in us. We are: helped, taught, reminded of God's grace and power, comforted, and given peace by the Holy Spirit *(John 14)*. In other words, we could not make it through the day without the Holy Spirit's presence.

It is time we truly embrace God the Holy Spirit. Let us fully come together on one accord and call upon the power of the Holy Spirit to move in our lives, and the life of the Church, like never before; let us be of the same faith and hope. The Book of Acts (2:41) states that about 3000 souls were added to the Church on this special day after Peter's message. Surely, we have been empowered by God to do even greater, if we ask in Jesus' name *(John 14:12-14)*.

Memorial Day

"You will keep him in perfect peace, whose mind is stayed on You, because he trusts in You."
(Isaiah 26:3)

As we reflect over the lives and loving relationships of our loved-ones passed on, it is my prayer peace will make its home in our hearts.

I am reminded of the terrorist acts our world has encountered, and the loved-ones that have been lost through acts of war; as well as the bigotry our own nation has demonstrated through the judicial system— justifying un-sustained acts of killings. I do not believe God is pleased with the behaviors displayed by terrorists, nor the nonchalant attitudes found in these United States. Attitudes of racism, sexism, greed and downright hate, run rapid from those in the public eye to those hiding behind the political issues of the day. There is no denying the divisive spirit of confusion and destruction in our nation; however, God is not the author of confusion, but peace *(1 Cor. 14:33)*.

If it is your desire to experience a peace that surpasses all understanding as you journey toward your destiny, allow me to encourage you to meditate on, and conform to, the above Scripture— keep your mind on Jesus, trust Him to intercede on your behalf in every situation, and believe there is nothing too hard for Him. If you take on this attitude of trust, you will experience the peace of God which surpasses all understanding, and His peace will guard your heart and mind *(Philippians 4:7)*.

Children's Day

The Second Sunday in June

"—Let the little children come to Me, and do not forbid them; for of such is the kingdom of God."
(Luke 18:16)

*I*n this land of democracy, we have attempted to acknowledge the importance of every aspect of the family; therefore, we mustn't forget our children. I believe the most inclusive of all three notable holiday celebrations, (Mother's, Father's and Children's) is Children's Day. For regardless of gender, we all were once children, which should make it easier for us to relate to their plights.

What do you remember about your childhood? We all have memories. I've heard some say they desire their children to have better childhoods than they experienced. There is nothing wrong with wanting our posterity to excel in areas we were unable, but I employ you to examine your definition of "better."

Many people associate "better" with materialistic things. This is a huge mistake. Material objects often take our eyes off Jesus. To be rich in things and poor in spirit makes a very unhappy (joyless) person. The most important thing that our parents could have given us is still the most important thing that we can give our children and future generations: LOVE— for Love never fails, and covers a multitude of sins.

Remember, "God so LOVED the world that He gave His only begotten Son …"

Father's Day

*"I will be a Father to you,
And you shall be My sons and daughters . . ."*
(2 Corinthians 6:18)

It is that marvelous time of the year again for us to give honor to the fathers in our lives. Be it in the home, church, or community, father figures have always provided the foundation for our earthly existence. Fathers set the stage for the way we think and view life in general— whether good, bad, or indifferent. From our political party affiliation to our interest in sports, I believe esteemed men in our lives, father figures, have influenced.

As children growing up, we believe our earthly fathers are the most powerful people in the world. To us, they seem superhuman; no problem was too big for them to solve ... then one day, we woke up to the devastating truth— they were human too. For many, facing this fact can be very difficult and some times, what was once trust is replaced with an unforgivable barrier of resentment, which may even have an adverse affect on the offspring's view of relationships and marriage.

In today's society, for various reasons, more and more of our children are growing up in homes without the presence of their biological fathers. It is almost an epidemic. But as Christians, we have been empowered to make a difference in the lives of all people. We must share the Good News with those who don't know that we have a Father who is all powerful; a Father who is so great that He made the world just for His children; a Father who is bigger than any problem that could ever confront us; a Father who loves us more than we love ourselves.

4th of July

"What then shall we say to these things? If God is for us, who can be against us?"
(Romans 8:31)

Do you know who you are in Christ Jesus?

It is traditional for us to celebrate this great Day of Independence, affectionately known as the "4th of July." What a wonderful time for reunions; friends and families spend quality time together reminiscing over days gone by, and enjoying various festivities.

The freedom many of us now perceive and enjoy is being jeopardized every day. In the African American community, freedom is a mirage for many; the truth is, slavery has popped up its ugly head incognito. We live in a system that thrives off institutionalized slavery. The target of this genocidal attack is mostly black males. Families become more dysfunctional every day that the God-fearing male and breadwinner is absent, and it appears the system is designed for such a fate. Therefore, the question of the day is, how can men become breadwinners when we live in a society that takes away this very right from those whose freedom to obtain a decent job has been denied because of past mistakes?

I believe Paul's letter to the Church of Rome contains the answer for us today. Although it appears there are many obstacles blocking our path to life and wholeness, as long as God is for us, we can claim the victory. Change has to come in this present penal system and God's Church must accept the challenge of becoming the agent of change.

Remember, in all of the challenges that may confront us, we are more than conquerors through Him who loved us *(Romans 8:37)*.

Labor Day

"—be steadfast, immovable, always abounding in the work of the Lord, knowing that your labor is not in vain ..."
(1 Corinthian 15:58)

Labor Day is a time to celebrate and reflect. It's wonderful to actually have a holiday which recognizes and rewards us for the hard work that we perform in the secular world, but for me, this day means so much more. Each year, this day is a reminder of my conversion, the day I surrendered my life to Christ.

At the age of eleven, I decided to search for God. There was a longing deep inside of me that only God could satisfy; as God would ordain, my church held a Revival the last Monday in August, and I told my mother I wanted to "get religion." I had no idea of what the next eight days would entail, nor can I pen it all in this devotion, but I can share the end results.

Revival was held an extra night because of one soul, mine. The adversary had been on his job of trying to convince me there was no God, and it appeared he was victorious.

The benediction was given; some of the saints walked out in defeat, others just stared at me with frustration, but this one mother walked over to me and said, "Child, I know the Lord done saved you. What's wrong? Can't you say it?" With these words, a rumbling emerged within my soul, my mouth flew open; I said, "I know I've been saved." Upon saying these words, I felt a freeness I had never experienced; the presence of the adversary was gone. The Holy Spirit set souls afire, starting with mine. I felt fire stirring up in my heart; racing through my hands and feet. As I began to cry, even the tears that I shed were hot. It felt as though steam was coming out of my eyes and ears. Before I knew what had happened, the whole church had been engulfed by the Holy Spirit, even in the ones that had attempted to leave. I had never witnessed anything like that before, nor have I witnessed anything like it since. It was truly a day worth the Labor!

Veterans Day

*"—Though war may rise against me,
in this I will be confident."*
(Psalm 27:3)

There have been hundreds of thousands of men and women who have served this great country in our armed forces. Today we pay special homage to each one of them. From World War I to Vietnam to Desert Storm to present day War on Terror. Against the odds, our soldiers marched into battle to protect those in harm's way, and we are grateful.

Therefore on this 11th Day of November, Let it be Known to the Veterans and Present Day Soldiers of these United States of America that:

We celebrate your Strength and Tenacity

We honor your Faith and Courage

And we thank God for your Commitment to Serve

It is our prayer that you will always remember you are loved and appreciated. Regardless of the challenges the war may have introduced into your lives, be confident that you have a God who will not forsake you. Trust God to strengthen your hearts— your labor has not been in vain.

Thanksgiving Day

*"Enter into His gates with thanksgiving,
and into His courts with praise. Be thankful
to Him, and bless His name."*
(Psalm 100:4)

What a wonderful blessing it is for us to embark upon another opportunity to remember and give thanks for all of the wonderful things God has done for us, as we celebrate another Thanksgiving Day. We have much to be thankful.

Whether we feast at our homes, or travel to be with family and friends; we enjoy the goodness of the Lord. So, while we find pleasure in the food and fellowship, let us always remember the One who has been more than gracious to us. Let us begin and end our day by giving thanks unto God, the Giver of every good and perfect gift. *(James 1:17)*

Every day should be a day of thanksgiving!

Advent

"Then the angel said . . . 'Do not be afraid, Mary, for you have found favor with God.'"
(Luke 1:30)

The sacred season of Advent brings with it miracles which are birthed through hope, peace, love and faith. The above Scripture reminds us of God's ability and desire to perform miracles in the lives of God's children, for it was nothing less than a miracle that Jesus was conceived in the womb of a virgin, whom God had found favor.

I believe God has at least one more miracle for each one of us during this Advent season; however, the question is, will we be ready when it shows up? Mary had no forewarning that she would be visited by an angel; nor, had she been given hint of being the chosen vessel to bring forth the greatest miracle ever— God, Incarnate. But there was something she had to do before the miracle was conceived— she had to accept God's Word via the angel and believe that it could be done, ("Let it be done to me according to your word." *−Luke 1:38*)

Will you join me in prayer this Advent season? Let us pray that when God sends our miracle(s), we will be able to receive, believe and respond with the words of Mary, "Let it be to us according to Your Word."

Christmas Day

"For what is our hope?"
(1 Thessalonians 2:19)

This morning, our hearts are filled with hope. Children hope to receive the items they placed on their Christmas lists. Parents hope to have been able to provide their children with presents that will make them happy. Spouses hope to present just the right gifts to ensure a smile and hug— the list goes on. Whether we acknowledge it or not, the primary reason most people look forward to Christmas is to give and receive gifts. There is nothing wrong with giving, for the Bible teaches us it is better to give than receive (Acts 20:35). The problem comes when we get so lost in the materialist world of "X"ing out the "Christ" in Christmas that we too, leave Him out.

As Christians, our hope should first and foremost be in the coming of the Lord. It is a wonderful blessing to celebrate our Savior's birth, but we must remember and prepare for His return. Sharing the Good News of salvation through the cross is the greatest gift we can give to a dying world. We must tell those who don't know, and remind those who do, that our hope is in the Resurrection of Jesus from the grave; thusly, laying the foundation of our faith. And it is because of His great sacrifice of giving Himself for our souls, we too shall live. Life after death for those whose hope is in the Lord is inevitable.

It is my hope and prayer, this day, you will receive everything you hope for in Christ Jesus. Have a Merry and blessed Christmas!

Shirley J. Inkton Bowers is a native of Arkansas. She resides in Little Rock; however, grew up in the town of Eudora. Shirley is the mother of three: Dawn Ja'Melle, Jessica Kathleen (Charles), and William Alan Irving; and grandmother of Dylynn Jo'Elle, Isaiah William, and Isaac Arnell. A noted writer, teacher, preacher, and inspirational speaker— God has anointed her to serve as Founder and CEO of **Diamonds in the Rough**, a holistic ministry which promotes self-worth; she presents and facilitates classes, seminars and conferences on various empowering topics.

Other gifts and graces God has bestowed throughout her life's journey include:

African Methodist Episcopal Church (AMEC):

Itinerant Elder

Arkansas Conference Christian Education Director

Member, AR Conference Board of Examiners

Chair, AR Conference Ministerial Efficiency Committee

Asst. Chair, AR Conference Women in Ministry (WIM)

President, L.R. District Quarterly Conference Union

AR Conference Church School Superintendent

1st Female to serve from the 12th Episcopal District as Co-Dean for the **J**oint **I**nstitute of **M**inisters (8th, 10th, & 12th Districts of the AMEC—2004)

1st Female Pastor in the AR Conference Elected General Conference Delegate (2004)

1st Female Pastor, Quinn Chapel, Little Rock

1st Female Pastor, Ward Chapel, Little Rock

1st Female Pastor, New Horizon, Little Rock

12th Episcopal District (Arkansas & Oklahoma) **Christian Education Director** (2006 - 2012)

Worship Director/Executive Board Member
Connectional AME Women in Ministry (2009-2012)

12th Episcopal District Representative to Order of the FLAME World Methodist Evangelism Conference Epworth By The Sea, St. Simons Island, GA (2006)

Member of the 12th Episcopal District Delegation that traveled to South Africa, visiting Lusaka and Livingstone, Zambia; Manzina, Swaziland; Maseru, Lesotho; Sun City and Johannesburg (2006)

Education

    Masters of Science in Education— Leadership
University of Central Arkansas, Conway, AR

    Florida Center of Theological Center

    Jackson Theological Seminary, North Little Rock, AR

    Bachelors of Science in Education Philander Smith College
Little Rock, AR

Certifications/License

    Church School & Christian Education
AMEC Certification

    George W. Truett Theological Seminary
Proclaimers Place Certification

    AR State Department of Education K – 12th
Special Education Instructor

    AR State Department of Education
Principal Certification

Honors/Memberships

    Miss Philander Smith College (1979-80)

    Delta Sigma Theta Sorority, Inc.
(Central Arkansas Alumnae Chapter)

    Women in Ministry

    Fellowship of Church Educators

    Order of the FLAME –World Methodist Evangelism

Shirley is grateful for all that God has allowed her to experience, but acknowledges her greatest blessing was bestowed upon her at the young age of 11— when she gave her life to Christ; she likens it to the "fire" in which the prophet Jeremiah testified. Her acceptance to God's Calling was not an easy one, but she is reminded over and over again that God's grace has been, is, and shall continue to be, sufficient to fulfill God's will for her life.

For Speaking Engagements, Contact Shirley at:
501-407-0177
diamondsintheroughministry@gmail.com
www.diamondsintheroughministry.com

Printed in the United States
By Bookmasters